Civil Liberties

OPPOSING VIEWPOINTS®

D0112935

OTHER BOOKS OF RELATED INTEREST

OPPOSING VIEWPOINTS SERIES

Abortion

American Values

America's Prisons

America's Victims

Biomedical Ethics

Censorship

Crime and Criminals

Criminal Justice

Culture Wars

Death and Dying

The Death Penalty

Discrimination

Education in America

Euthanasia

Feminism

Gun Control

Hate Groups

Homosexuality

Human Rights

Illegal Immigration

Immigration

Inequality: Opposing Viewpoints
in Social Problems

Interracial America

The Legal System

Mass Media

Media Violence

Pornography

Race Relations

Social Justice

Suicide

The War on Drugs

CURRENT CONTROVERSIES SERIES

The Abortion Controversy

Assisted Suicide

Computers and Society

The Disabled

Ethics

Free Speech

Gay Rights

Gun Control

Hate Crimes

Illegal Immigration

Minorities

Native American Rights

Police Brutality

Racism

Violence in the Media

Women in the Military

AT ISSUE SERIES

Affirmative Action

Anti-Semitism

The Future of the Internet

Gay Marriage

Immigration Policy

The Jury System

Legalizing Drugs

Physician-Assisted Suicide

Civil Liberties

OPPOSING VIEWPOINTS®

David L. Bender, *Publisher*
Bruno Leone, *Executive Editor*
Bonnie Szumski, *Editorial Director*
Brenda Stalcup, *Managing Editor*
Scott Barbour, *Senior Editor*
Tamara L. Roleff, *Book Editor*

OPPOSING
VIEWPOINTS®
SERIES

Greenhaven Press, Inc., San Diego, California

Cover photo: Craig MacLain

Library of Congress Cataloging-in-Publication Data

Civil liberties : opposing viewpoints / Tamara L. Roleff, book editor.
    p.   cm. — (Opposing viewpoints series)
    Includes bibliographical references and index.
    ISBN 1-56510-936-8 (pbk. : alk. paper). — ISBN 1-56510-937-6
(lib. : alk. paper)
    1. Civil rights—United States. I. Roleff, Tamara L., 1959–   .
II. Series: Opposing viewpoints series (Unnumbered)
KF4749.A2C497 1999

                                                          98-11808
                                                              CIP

Greenhaven Press, Inc., P.O. Box 289009
San Diego, CA 92198-9009

"CONGRESS SHALL MAKE NO LAW... ABRIDGING THE FREEDOM OF SPEECH, OR OF THE PRESS."

First Amendment to the U.S. Constitution

The basic foundation of our democracy is the First Amendment guarantee of freedom of expression. The Opposing Viewpoints Series is dedicated to the concept of this basic freedom and the idea that it is more important to practice it than to enshrine it.

CONTENTS

Why Consider Opposing Viewpoints?   9

Introduction   12

Chapter 1: Should Limits Be Placed on Freedom of Expression?

Chapter Preface   16

1. Free Speech Should Be Restricted   17
   Mark Y. Herring

2. Free Speech Should Not Be Restricted   22
   Mark Turiano

3. Hate Speech Should Be Restricted   27
   Richard Delgado and David Yun

4. Hate Speech Should Not Be Restricted   36
   American Civil Liberties Union

5. Flag Burning as Political Speech Should
   Be Restricted   44
   Richard Parker

6. Flag Burning as Political Speech Should Not
   Be Restricted   52
   Part I: Roger Pilon, Part II: Carole Shields

7. The Government Should Legislate Against
   Pornography   59
   Catherine Itzin

8. Pornography Should Not Be Restricted   65
   Nadine Strossen

Periodical Bibliography   70

Chapter 2: Is the Right to Privacy Threatened?

Chapter Preface   72

1. A Loss of Privacy Benefits Society   73
   Amitai Etzioni

2. A Loss of Privacy Harms Society   77
   Joseph S. Fulda

3. More Laws Are Needed to Protect Privacy   81
   Cass R. Sunstein

4. More Laws Are Not Needed to Protect Privacy   85
   Jane E. Kirtley

5. Random Drug Tests on Student-Athletes Do
   Not Violate the Right to Privacy 89
   Antonin Scalia et al.

6. Random Drug Tests on Student-Athletes Violate
   the Right to Privacy 98
   Sandra Day O'Connor, John Paul Stevens, and David Souter

7. Wiretaps Violate the Right to Privacy 107
   Laura W. Murphy

8. Wiretaps Are Necessary to Fight Crime 112
   David Gelernter

Periodical Bibliography 117

Chapter 3: Should Church and State Be Separate?

Chapter Preface 119

1. The Constitution's Framers Intended Strict
   Separation of Church and State 120
   Baptist Joint Committee on Public Affairs

2. The Constitution's Framers Did Not Intend
   Strict Separation of Church and State 128
   M. Stanton Evans

3. School Prayer Threatens Religious Liberty 138
   Roger Simon

4. Prohibiting School Prayer Threatens Religious
   Liberty 142
   Linda Bowles

5. Tax Dollars Should Not Fund Religious Schools 146
   Bob Peterson

6. Tax Dollars Should Fund Religious Schools 153
   Denis P. Doyle

Periodical Bibliography 159

**Chapter 4: How Does the Internet Affect Civil
Liberties?**

Chapter Preface 161

1. The Internet Threatens the Right to Privacy 162
   Nathaniel Sheppard Jr.

2. The Internet's Invasion of Privacy Is Exaggerated 166
   Joseph Burns

3. Indecent Material on the Internet Should Be
   Censored 169
   Shyla Welch

4. Censoring Indecent Material on the Internet
   Violates Free Speech   174
   American Civil Liberties Union
5. Computer Encryption Threatens Public Safety   183
   Robert S. Litt
6. Computer Encryption Codes Are Necessary
   to Protect Privacy   189
   Part I: *Peter Wayner*, Part II: *James P. Lucier*

Periodical Bibliography   195

For Further Discussion   196
Organizations to Contact   198
Bibliography of Books   201
Index   203

WHY CONSIDER
OPPOSING VIEWPOINTS?

*"The only way in which a human being can make some
approach to knowing the whole of a subject is by hearing
what can be said about it by persons of every variety of
opinion and studying all modes in which it can be looked
at by every character of mind. No wise man ever acquired
his wisdom in any mode but this."*

John Stuart Mill

In our media-intensive culture it is not difficult to find differing
opinions. Thousands of newspapers and magazines and dozens
of radio and television talk shows resound with differing points
of view. The difficulty lies in deciding which opinion to agree
with and which "experts" seem the most credible. The more in-
undated we become with differing opinions and claims, the
more essential it is to hone critical reading and thinking skills to
evaluate these ideas. Opposing Viewpoints books address this
problem directly by presenting stimulating debates that can be
used to enhance and teach these skills. The varied opinions contained in each book examine many different aspects of a single
issue. While examining these conveniently edited opposing
views, readers can develop critical thinking skills such as the
ability to compare and contrast authors' credibility, facts, argu-
mentation styles, use of persuasive techniques, and other stylis-
tic tools. In short, the Opposing Viewpoints Series is an ideal
way to attain the higher-level thinking and reading skills so essential in a culture of diverse and contradictory opinions.

In addition to providing a tool for critical thinking, Opposing
Viewpoints books challenge readers to question their own
strongly held opinions and assumptions. Most people form their
opinions on the basis of upbringing, peer pressure, and personal, cultural, or professional bias. By reading carefully balanced opposing views, readers must directly confront new ideas
as well as the opinions of those with whom they disagree. This
is not to simplistically argue that everyone who reads opposing
views will—or should—change his or her opinion. Instead, the
series enhances readers' understanding of their own views by
encouraging confrontation with opposing ideas. Careful examination of others' views can lead to the readers' understanding of
the logical inconsistencies in their own opinions, perspective on

why they hold an opinion, and the consideration of the possibility that their opinion requires further evaluation.

EVALUATING OTHER OPINIONS

To ensure that this type of examination occurs, Opposing Viewpoints books present all types of opinions. Prominent spokespeople on different sides of each issue as well as well-known professionals from many disciplines challenge the reader. An additional goal of the series is to provide a forum for other, less known, or even unpopular viewpoints. The opinion of an ordinary person who has had to make the decision to cut off life support from a terminally ill relative, for example, may be just as valuable and provide just as much insight as a medical ethicist's professional opinion. The editors have two additional purposes in including these less known views. One, the editors encourage readers to respect others' opinions—even when not enhanced by professional credibility. It is only by reading or listening to and objectively evaluating others' ideas that one can determine whether they are worthy of consideration. Two, the inclusion of such viewpoints encourages the important critical thinking skill of objectively evaluating an author's credentials and bias. This evaluation will illuminate an author's reasons for taking a particular stance on an issue and will aid in readers' evaluation of the author's ideas.

As series editors of the Opposing Viewpoints Series, it is our hope that these books will give readers a deeper understanding of the issues debated and an appreciation of the complexity of even seemingly simple issues when good and honest people disagree. This awareness is particularly important in a democratic society such as ours in which people enter into public debate to determine the common good. Those with whom one disagrees should not be regarded as enemies but rather as people whose views deserve careful examination and may shed light on one's own.

Thomas Jefferson once said that "difference of opinion leads to inquiry, and inquiry to truth." Jefferson, a broadly educated man, argued that "if a nation expects to be ignorant and free . . . it expects what never was and never will be." As individuals and as a nation, it is imperative that we consider the opinions of others and examine them with skill and discernment. The Opposing Viewpoints Series is intended to help readers achieve this goal.

David L. Bender & Bruno Leone,
Series Editors

Greenhaven Press anthologies primarily consist of previously published material taken from a variety of sources, including periodicals, books, scholarly journals, newspapers, government documents, and position papers from private and public organizations. These original sources are often edited for length and to ensure their accessibility for a young adult audience. The anthology editors also change the original titles of these works in order to clearly present the main thesis of each viewpoint and to explicitly indicate the opinion presented in the viewpoint. These alterations are made in consideration of both the reading and comprehension levels of a young adult audience. Every effort is made to ensure that Greenhaven Press accurately reflects the original intent of the authors included in this anthology.

INTRODUCTION

"For those who value free expression, it is worth remembering that sticks and stones may break your bones, but e-mails will never hurt you."
—Kenneth Lake, Internet Freedom News, February 13, 1998

"High-tech hate is not going to be tolerated. A line does have to be drawn in the world of cyberspace. If you cross that line ... you are going to be subject to criminal penalties."
—Michael J. Gennaco

In September 1996, fifty-nine Asian students at the University of California in Irvine turned on their computers to find that someone had sent them an e-mail message blaming them for all the crimes committed on campus. If the students did not quit school, the writer warned, "I personally will make it my life career to find and kill every one of you personally."

Although some of the students shrugged off the e-mail as a joke, others were concerned enough that they started carrying pepper spray, stopped going out at night, and became suspicious of strangers. The identity of the sender was easily determined to be Richard Machado, a former student at UCI. Machado believed that Asian students were responsible for raising the grading curve, thereby causing him to flunk out of school.

The Internet is such a new and different entity that few laws govern its use. Machado's case was one of the earliest to test the limits of free speech on the Internet. His first trial, in November 1997, resulted in a mistrial with the jury deadlocked nine to three in favor of acquittal. He was convicted at his second trial, in February 1998, of just one charge: "interfering" with the students' right to attend the university—a federal crime under the civil rights laws enacted during the 1960s. After the trial, assistant U.S. attorney Michael J. Gennaco vowed to prosecute other computer users who stalk or threaten people over the Internet.

Due to the rapid growth of the Internet, more people than ever before are exposed to hate and racist speech. Hate groups find establishing a website easier and less costly than the more traditional means of spreading their message, such as flyers and mass mailings. The number of websites promoting racist or hate speech is estimated to have doubled in the 1990s to between five hundred and six hundred sites. Hate speech and racist material are also available in other forums on the Internet, such as newsgroups, electronic bulletin boards, and chat rooms, which increases the chances that people will come across violent and racist speech while browsing the Internet.)

[Those who favor banning "cyber hate speech" maintain that racist propaganda and hate material can harm and distress not only the intended recipients but also others who may come across it accidentally. Meeka Jun writes in the *New York Law Journal*, "When threats are sent by telephone or regular mail, the harm is usually limited to a single victim. When threats are sent through the Internet, the harm can spread quickly to injure widespread audiences." Minorities, women, homosexuals, and the disabled are the usual targets of hate speech. A vast number of these people can be affected by just one e-mail message or a racist or hate speech website. Therefore, proponents of a hate speech ban assert, just as speech that incites a riot is illegal, speech that advocates hatred or violence against a person or group should also be illegal, especially if it appears on the Internet, where it may affect a great many people.

Opponents of hate speech also contend that the inflammatory words inherent in the speech could easily lead to violent behavior. They maintain that if the sender's intent is to cause fear of injury or to incite violence—as was charged in the Machado case—then the speech must be prohibited. Richard Delgado and David Yun, write, "Once the speaker identifies someone as being in the category of deserved victim, his or her behavior toward that person is likely to escalate from reviling to bullying and physical violence." Therefore, they conclude, in order to protect innocent people from potential harm, racist propaganda and hate speech must be prohibited.)

(Such a prohibition would not violate the First Amendment's guarantee of freedom of speech, Delgado and Yun maintain, because many types of speech are already legally restricted. For example, the right to falsely yell "fire" in a crowded theater is not protected by the First Amendment because of the potential harm it could cause. Therefore, they assert, banning hate speech that could lead to physical harm for the person being denigrated is not a violation of the right to free speech, either.)

[Machado's lawyer and civil libertarians disagree, however. They argue that as distasteful as it may be, hate speech is protected under the First Amendment. Banning or regulating hate speech—whether on the Internet or not—violates the right to freedom of speech, they assert. Websites on the Internet that espouse hate speech are protected, they point out, and therefore

Machado's hate e-mail should also be protected.

Machado's defense was that his hate e-mail was a "stupid prank" that should not have been taken seriously. According to an Internet etiquette expert witness, Machado's angry message was "a classic flame," an on-line term for an inflammatory message on the Internet that is not meant to cause actual harm. Furthermore, censorship opponents assert, hate speech consists merely of words, and there is a clear line between words and actions. As Kenneth Lake of the *Internet Freedom News* argues,

> For some time there has been an authoritarian shift in the focus of criminal law from deed to word to thought. . . . In Machado's case, the only "act" was the sending of a threatening e-mail. The criminalisation of e-mail indicates the continuing expansion of the category of mental crime.

In Lake's opinion, criminalizing hate e-mail will lead to criminalizing the motive behind it, soon making it a crime to hate.

Civil libertarians also maintain that permitting hate groups to display their racism on the Internet allows anti-hate groups—those who oppose the principles espoused by hate groups—to monitor them more easily. Anti-hate groups can counter the offensive material with more speech that exposes the hate groups' falsehoods, errors in logic, and other mistakes, explains Stanton McCandlish of the Electronic Frontier Foundation. For instance, Frank Xavier Placencia started his own Internet website called Hate Page of the Week. According to Placencia, the purpose of the website is "to remind us that there is still a great deal of hatred in this world, that racism and anti-Semitism remain great threats to our society." Don Haines, an attorney with the American Civil Liberties Union, has another remedy for fighting cyber hate speech that does not violate the First Amendment. "When confronted with offensive material on-line, a person can simply shut off the computer and it is gone."

The Machado trial over hate speech on the Internet symbolizes the difficulty in balancing an individual's right to exercise a civil liberty—be it freedom of speech, freedom of religion, or the right to privacy—against society's right to be protected from harm. In *Civil Liberties: Opposing Viewpoints*, the authors examine civil liberty issues in the following chapters: Should Limits Be Placed on Freedom of Expression? Is the Right to Privacy Threatened? Should Church and State Be Separate? How Does the Internet Affect Civil Liberties? As the viewpoints contained in these chapters reveal, the very nature of civil liberties requires a never-ending balancing act between the rights of the individual and the universal rights of society.

CHAPTER 1

SHOULD LIMITS BE PLACED ON FREEDOM OF EXPRESSION?

CHAPTER PREFACE

In April 1996, Oprah Winfrey hosted a talk show about the possible emergence of mad cow disease in the United States. The infectious agent of mad cow disease (which is thought to be caused by feeding cattle the ground-up carcasses of infected sheep or cows) eats a hole in the brain of both cows and people who eat the infected beef. At least twenty deaths in England were attributed to the human equivalent of mad cow disease, Creuzfeldt-Jakob disease, in 1996. After a food safety activist advised how the disease is spread, Winfrey exclaimed, "It has just stopped me cold from eating another burger!" When Winfrey's show aired, cattle prices dropped dramatically and continued to fall for two weeks.

After Winfrey's show, Paul Engler, a Texas cattle rancher who contends he lost $6.7 million in the "Oprah Crash of '96," sued Winfrey in federal court under the state's "veggie libel laws." Veggie libel laws, such as Texas's False Disparagement of Perishable Food Products Act, are meant to protect food products from false or disparaging remarks. Engler charged that Winfrey's remarks spread alarmist and false information about American beef and that she should be held accountable for the cattle industry's financial losses.

Civil liberties attorneys, however, argue that veggie libel laws violate freedom of speech and can be used to silence health and safety warnings. Unfettered debate is essential to protect the health and safety of consumers, they assert. If veggie libel laws are permitted to stand, they contend, the restrictions on free speech could stifle important scientific findings similar to those that warned consumers about the dangers of cigarette smoking, cancer-causing agents in foods, and the possibility of E. coli infections from some fast-food outlets.

Although Winfrey's 1998 acquittal was unanimous, the argument over free speech versus false disparagement was not fully settled. Midway through Winfrey's trial, the judge ruled that the cattlemen could not pursue damage claims under the veggie libel laws but must sue under the more difficult-to-prove business defamation laws. The constitutionality of veggie libel laws remains undecided. The fate of these laws will affect other free speech issues, such as whether pornography, flag burning, or hate speech should also be limited. The authors in the following chapter examine whether these restrictions threaten freedom of speech.

"If you care about the quality of life,
... you have to be in favor of some
form of censorship."

FREE SPEECH SHOULD BE RESTRICTED

Mark Y. Herring

In the following viewpoint, Mark Y. Herring argues that the Founding Fathers did not intend for free speech to be absolute with no restrictions. It is possible, he contends, to protect intellectual freedom while still censoring obscene or indecent material. The current policy of permitting unrestrained speech in the name of the First Amendment is threatening to destroy society, Herring asserts. Herring is the dean of library services at Oklahoma Baptist University in Shawnee.

As you read, consider the following questions:

1. What is Irving Kristol's philosophy concerning censorship, as cited by Herring?
2. According to the author, which historic figures supported restrictions on free speech?
3. In which areas did John Milton advocate censorship, according to Herring?

Reprinted from Mark Y. Herring, "Cybersex," St. Croix Review, October 1995, by permission of the St. Croix Review.

I have had the pleasure of serving on the executive board of my state's library association. Amid the usual bureaucratic nonsense such committees are heir to, came a not-so-bureaucratic one dealing with intellectual freedom. Our state legislature, our legislative liaison reported, wished to prohibit publicly funded computer access to Internet sites offering the "obscene, filthy, indecent, lascivious, lewd or unfit."

Yes, many in the room did begin to hyperventilate. Having been an academic librarian for more than a decade and a half, I have enjoyed watching the vicissitudes of academia with respect to intellectual freedom. But none have been more prepossessing to witness than from the coign of vantage of a practicing librarian. Prepossessing? Let me clarify that: a practicing librarian who opposes unbridled intellectual freedom, i.e., the kind of intellectual freedom endorsed by the American Library Association (ALA). I've always believed that if you care about the quality of life, as Irving Kristol once put it, you have to be in favor of some form of censorship.

AN UNORTHODOX VIEW

Such an admission in academic circles is not merely unorthodox the way, say, it would be if Ted Kennedy admitted he listened to Rush Limbaugh. It's far more apocalyptic than that. It's really more on the order of [former National Organization for Women president] Pat Ireland saying she really prefers to stay home and bake cookies while barefooted and pregnant: my position is unheard of among academics. The official position of academia is that intellectual freedom should be unrestrained. But the official position of ALA outdoes it by a half: censorship of any kind for any reason about any matter whatever is wrong. Period. End of argument.

If you don't believe me, here are the Association's own words:

> In basic terms, intellectual freedom means the right of any person to believe what he wants on any subject, and to express his beliefs or ideas in whatever way he thinks appropriate. (ALA's *Intellectual Freedom Manual*)

Examine the statement carefully: ". . . whatever way he thinks appropriate." Later, the *Manual* leaves no room for doubt, declaring that the freedom of ideas means expressing them "in any mode of communication." That this gives carte blanche not only to pornographers and "performance artists" of every stripe is unmistakable; that it gives free rein to every [serial killer] Son-of-Sam is undeniable. The intent of the *Manual* is clear: censorship for any reason is bad, wrong, ugly, and immoral. It's not neat either.

In a nutshell, the Oklahoma state legislature wanted to avoid having taxpayers pay for cybersex; the voyeurism of those who might want to connect with "900" Internet numbers on a graphical interface. They weren't outlawing them, mind you, just outlawing public funding of them. And all at once, everyone in the room thought the Constitution had begun to crumble. Well, almost everyone.

SPEECH THAT SHOULD BE RESTRICTED

A poll of 1,026 Americans taken between July 17 and August 1, 1997, found that 93 percent would vote for the First Amendment if it were being ratified in 1997. However, according to those polled, some forms of speech should be restricted:

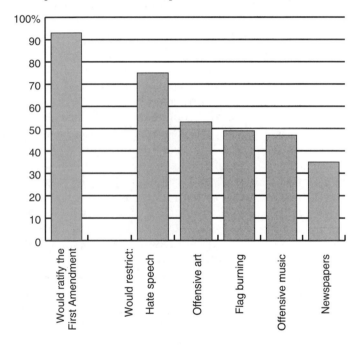

Source: Center for Survey Research and Analysis, 1997.

The motion to oppose the bill on record passed with only one dissenting vote: mine. When I indicated to the committee that as information gatekeepers we had better know the difference between "obscene, filthy, indecent, lascivious, lewd or unfit" information, and information that was not, all I got back were bland stares. From what planet did I come from?

But the more important question is, where did this idea of

unbridled, unrestrained, intellectual freedom come from? How is it that if you censor, say, cybersex fellatio, our Constitution ends in shambles?

The Dutch philosopher Baruch Spinoza restricted speech out of anger; John Locke against moral strictures that preserved civilized society. Even Thomas Jefferson allowed restraint against public opinion. Only John Stuart Mill comes closest to this absolutist view, but even he allowed for censorship when it might do harm to others. Even though Mill's view of liberty is the most absolutist, his is not as absolutist as the modern, academic one.

Librarians and academics alike delight in referencing John Milton's *Areopagitica* but this is because they do not read it, or do not read it carefully enough. Milton restricted where moderns are especially eager to, in areas of "popery" (i.e., religion), and in areas where they are loathe to, superstition (it's superior to religion, as the pagan artifact erected in a San Jose, California city park indicates). Finally, our Founding Fathers never intended that the First Amendment be taken to mean that any and all modes of communication should be unrestrained and readily accessible. Yet we moderns think that liberty must be absolute or it cannot be liberty at all. We seem either unable, unwilling, or a little of both, to make any intellectual distinction between liberty on the one hand, and libertinage on the other.

The very underpinnings of the idea of intellectual freedom—mental freedom, if you will—being absolutist in nature, is a wholly modern idea, with virtually no historical foundation other than Mill's qualified absolutism. Hasn't history proven its dictum in spades that what is not learned in one age is repeated in the next? For who can deny Baron de Montesquieu's charge that when egalitarianism becomes a mania, license replaces virtue? Or, more simply, when virtue is no longer encouraged publicly, it is no longer practiced privately. Walter Lippman had it precisely when he wrote, "Freedom of speech separated from its essential principle leads through a short, transitional chaos to the destruction of freedom of speech."

A FINE LINE

Of course instituting some level of censoriousness regarding public behavior opens us up to a level of danger. It is a fine line between sensible censorship and an outright restriction of basic liberties, as James Bovard's book, *Lost Rights*, clearly indicates. But it isn't so narrow as tightrope walking, and does not require professional funambulists to do it. Surely our present culture is evidence enough that the course we have charted for ourselves since 1970 threatens to undo, not only us, but the very republic we love so dearly.

I cannot say whether either librarians or academics will ever learn that liberty and libertinage are two different matters. Both appear hell-bent on destroying this culture, trying to prove they are synonymous. But I can, however, tell you this much. When I raised these same issues while serving another state library association, I was greeted with a response that has amused me ever since: the members voted to censure me.

| "Freedom of speech is connected to human excellence."

FREE SPEECH SHOULD NOT BE RESTRICTED

Mark Turiano

Freedom of speech is necessary in order for cultures to achieve greatness, Mark Turiano maintains in the following viewpoint. Free speech preserves liberty by preventing the spread of uncontrollable power, he asserts. Tolerating offensive speech is the sign of a morally mature and virtuous person, he contends, qualities that are necessary to sustain a free and open society. Turiano is a freelance writer near Atlanta, Georgia.

As you read, consider the following questions:
1. According to Turiano, how does freedom of speech check the arbitrary use of power?
2. How does free speech encourage the development of virtue, in the author's opinion?
3. How does Turiano define "toleration" as related to freedom of speech?

Reprinted from Mark Turiano, "The Virtues of Free Speech," The Freeman, September 1996, by permission of The Freeman.

If all mankind minus one, were of one opinion, and only one person were of the contrary opinion, mankind would be no more justified in silencing that one person, than he, if he had the power, would be justified in silencing mankind.

—John Stuart Mill, *On Liberty*

A ny persuasive argument for liberty must involve a connection between liberty and human excellence. The reason for this is clear. An argument for liberty is an argument for its goodness. The ultimate context for all human evaluation of good news is human life. To ask if liberty is good is to seek a connection between it and human goodness or excellence.

Does freedom of speech have any value if we take human excellence seriously? I think so. First of all, freedom of speech has a value in the realm of political economy. The ability to speak one's mind concerning matters of common interest is useful insofar as it helps preserve a more general freedom. A power that is not open to the scrutiny and conscientious objections of those over whom it is exercised is almost certain to be exercised irrationally. The price of liberty, to paraphrase John Philpot Curran, is eternal vigilance. Freedom of speech in this political sense preserves a sphere for the exercise of that vigilance. Freedom of speech is of instrumental value to a jealous love of liberty, without which, freedom of speech is completely impotent. Freedom of speech concerning political matters is worth preserving because it acts as a check against the arbitrary use of power.

PRESERVING NONPOLITICAL SPEECH

However, considered merely as a political tool, freedom of speech is quite limited. It can only be understood to have a bearing on matters that are of common concern. This is quite compatible with a severe repression of speech about private matters. Freedom of speech in this sense could involve my freedom to exhort my neighbors into barring the opening of an X-rated theater in our neighborhood, or in the suppression of the use of foul language. The question then is can there be a justification for expanding freedom of speech to these other areas? Such a justification must show that the protection of certain types of speech in other, nonpolitical, areas (e.g., the arts and sciences) has a connection to human excellence. And it seems that it does; scientific and artistic achievement seem to be fostered by freedom.

How far ought this freedom to extend? The description of sexual function by biologists can be clearly connected to the advancement of learning and maybe even to the curing of disease or preservation of life. The depiction of violence in some art-works might be justified for its cathartic effect. When, for example, Mel Gibson is being disemboweled in *Braveheart* and refuses to submit as an act of defiance to tyranny, this serves primarily as a representation of fortitude and strength of spirit, and only secondarily as a depiction of human cruelty. The cruelty is conquered by the virtue and is overshadowed by it.

WHY FREE SPEECH IS ESSENTIAL TO A FREE SOCIETY

[Free speech is] vital to the attainment and advancement of knowledge, and the search for the truth. The eminent 19th-century writer and civil libertarian, John Stuart Mill, contended that enlightened judgment is possible only if one considers all facts and ideas, from whatever source, and tests one's own conclusions against opposing views. Therefore, all points of view—even those that are "bad" or socially harmful—should be represented in society's "marketplace of ideas."

It's necessary to our system of self-government and gives the American people a "checking function" against government excess and corruption. If the American people are to be the masters of their fate and of their elected government, they must be well-informed and have access to all information, ideas and points of view. Mass ignorance is a breeding ground for oppression and tyranny.

American Civil Liberties Union, "Freedom of Expression," Briefing Paper Number 10, 1997.

What then of the obscene ranting of rap musicians glorifying disregard for law and common decency? Or books and films in which people are senselessly murdered by the sociopathic protagonists, or those which amount to character assassinations of well-known individuals based on outright lies and half-truths? Can there be any justification of these things?

VIRTUE

Two arguments can be made. First, human excellence is most fully manifest in what we might call a morally mature person. This is a person who manifests all of the classical virtues, including courage, prudence, and justice. Now virtue, as such, cannot be compelled, though people can be compelled (that is, forced against their own judgment) to behave in the same way that a virtuous person would. Such behavior is not an expression of virtue. Virtue requires freedom to act in light of one's own judgment. Granted, certain types of self-expression are defective, but to prohibit them, and thus force people to behave as if they were virtuous, will not make them actually virtuous, since the element of judgment and choice is removed. There are cases where we are justified in compelling people to behave as if they were virtuous. Parents do this to their children in the hope that the children will, by so acting, become virtuous. This is the moral equivalent of putting training wheels on a bicycle.

To treat an adult this way is to treat him as if he were not only without virtue but so defective in this regard that force rather than reason is required. Someone who is less than completely virtuous can be persuaded and shamed into behaving and may, given time, actually develop virtue. For example, someone who desires to produce a movie which plausibly presents his fantasies as if they were true, and in so doing dishonors the memory and reputation of a former president, might be dissuaded by means of reason or shame. Using such means is an acknowledgment of a capacity for virtue and is the best means of inculcating it. If because of irrationality or shamelessness, he persists, stronger measures might be called for. Such measures would be in place particularly if significant and foreseeable harm was caused.

The bottom line is that since moral maturity requires the freedom to act according to one's judgment, such freedom should be granted except in extreme cases. The authority of virtue is quite different from the authority of strength. Forcing someone to do or refrain from doing something tends to obscure the beauty of the same action when it is done from virtue. Because freedom, including freedom of speech, favors the development of virtue, it is valuable and ought to be preserved.

MORALITY

There is another persuasive argument that can be made in favor of freedom of speech. Though this is more of a cultural than a political argument, it is based on the vast difference between being moral and being a moralist. The morally mature person—the virtuous individual—seeks always to do that which is noble and praiseworthy. In doing so, he becomes the standard of moral excellence. The moralist is the person who, in lieu of noble and praiseworthy actions, seeks merely to condemn the base and shameful. The moral man only condemns vice insofar as virtue requires it, the moralist only acts virtuously (or seems to) in order to retain the right to condemn vice.

Toleration is an attitude that acts as a check against moralism.

It should be noted that toleration is not the morally skeptical refusal to make judgments and to condemn certain types of behavior or speech. Rather, it is the recognition that such judgments should be made only when and to the extent that some good may come of them. Whereas a moralist takes pleasure in the mere condemnation of shameful behavior, a tolerant person finds such condemnation distasteful and can only make it palatable to himself if he can combine it with some noble action. The moralist is mean-spirited, the man of virtue is magnanimous. A tolerant culture is one which encourages the virtue of magnanimity or greatness of mind.

To Tolerate or Not?

It is not possible from one's armchair to say exactly what types of speech would be tolerated in such a culture, and it is probably not even possible to arrive at universal criteria for which types of speech should be tolerated. The types of sexually explicit material, for example, that ought to be tolerated in New York City are probably not the same as those that should be tolerated in Opelika, Alabama. The point is that whatever they are, such forms of speech would be *tolerated*, i.e., they would be put up with although they are acknowledged to be base or defective in some way. This toleration would not be based on the hidden, subjective value of what is tolerated, on some moral skepticism which relativizes all values, or on some right to express oneself. Instead, it would be based on the recognition that to use force to restrain such speech would be pointless or ineffective for inculcating virtue and would be out of proportion to the smallness of the act. It would be out of revulsion at the mean-spiritedness involved in such a use of force that it would be tolerated.

It seems then that freedom of speech is connected to human excellence in several ways. Politically, freedom of speech is useful for the protection of freedom to act in as much as it acts as a check against arbitrary power. As one type of freedom it can also aid in the development of virtue by opening up a sphere in which one can act according to one's judgment. Such freedom is necessary for virtue. It is culturally useful for the development of the arts and sciences, and, finally, because it requires toleration, it fosters greatness of soul.

"Targeted racial vilification [does not] promote any of the theoretical rationales for protecting free speech."

HATE SPEECH SHOULD BE RESTRICTED

Richard Delgado and David Yun

In the following viewpoint, Richard Delgado and David Yun contend that arguments for permitting hate speech are paternalistic and seriously flawed. They argue that allowing hate speech tends to worsen the overall situation for minority groups. In addition, the authors assert that it is oftentimes impossible or dangerous for minority members to try to respond to hate speech directed at them. Therefore, the authors maintain, minorities need protection from hate speech. Delgado is the Charles Inglis Thomson Professor of Law at the University of Colorado. Yun is an attorney in Colorado.

As you read, consider the following questions:
1. What are the four arguments for permitting hate speech, according to the authors?
2. In Delgado and Yun's opinion, why does the reverse enforcement argument against hate speech have little validity?
3. According to the authors, why is it often dangerous or impossible for victims of hate speech to respond to such speech?

Reprinted from Richard Delgado and David Yun, "Pressure Valves and Bloodied Chickens: An Assessment of Four Paternalistic Arguments for Resisting Hate-Speech, Hate Propaganda, and Pornography," *California Law Review*, vol. 82, no. 4 (1994), pp. 871–92, by permission; ©1994 by California Law Review, Inc.

Beginning around 1979, many campuses began noticing a rise in the number of incidents of hate-ridden speech directed at minorities, gays, lesbians, and others. At the University of California at Berkeley, for example, a fraternity member shouted obscenities and racial slurs at a group of black students as they passed his house; later, a disc jockey told black students to "go back to Oakland" when they asked the campus station to play rap music. At Stanford, when black students insisted that Beethoven was a mulatto, some white students denied it and publicly defaced a poster of the composer by scribbling stereotypically black facial features on it. At the University of Massachusetts, postgame racial tensions exploded in a brawl that left a number of students injured. According to the *Chronicle of Higher Education*, nearly 200 institutions of higher learning have experienced racial unrest serious enough to be reported in the news. The National Institute Against Prejudice and Violence estimates that at least 20 percent of minority students are victimized at least once during their college years.

Experts are divided on both the causes and the believability of this apparent upsurge in campus racism. A few argue that there is no such increase—that the numbers are the result of better reporting or heightened social sensitivities. Most, however, believe the change is real, noting that it is a part of a steady rise in attacks on foreigners, immigrants, and ethnic minorities under way in many Western industrialized nations. These events may reflect deteriorating economies and increasing competition for jobs, growth in populations of color stemming from immigration patterns and a high birthrate, the ending of the cold war, or all of these.

A MAJOR CONCERN

Whatever its cause, campus racism is a major concern for educators and university officials. At the University of Wisconsin, for example, black enrollment dropped sharply in the wake of highly publicized incidents of campus racism. Finding themselves faced with this kind of negative publicity and declining minority numbers, many institutions established campus programs aimed at racial awareness. Others broadened their curriculum to include more multicultural offerings and events. Still others enacted hate speech codes that prohibit slurs and disparaging remarks directed against persons on account of their ethnicity, religion, or sexual orientation. Sometimes these are patterned after existing torts or the "fighting words" exception to the First Amendment. One, at the University of Texas, bars personalized insults that amount to intentional infliction of emotional distress. Another, at the University of California at Berkeley, prohibits "those personally abusive epithets which directly addressed to any ordinary person, are likely to provoke a violent reaction whether or not they actually do so.". . .

PATERNALISTIC JUSTIFICATIONS

Much of the debate over hate speech rules has moved from issues of constitutionality to ones of policy. Central to this debate are four paternalistic arguments made by opponents of antiracism rules; each invokes the interest of the group seeking protection. The four arguments are:

1. Permitting racists to utter racist remarks and insults allows them to blow off steam harmlessly. As a consequence, minorities are safer than they would be under a regime of antiracism rules. We will refer to this as the "pressure valve" argument.

2. Enacting antiracism rules will end up hurting minorities because authorities will apply the rules against them, rather than against members of the majority group. This we will call the reverse enforcement argument.

3. Free speech has been minorities' best friend. It is a principal instrument of social reform, so, as persons interested in achieving reform, minorities should resist placing any fetters on freedom of expression. This we term the "best friend" objection.

4. More speech—talking back to the aggressor—is the solution to racist speech. Talking back is more empowering than regulation. It strengthens one's identity, reduces victimization, and instills pride in one's heritage. This we term the "talk back" argument.

We believe each of these arguments to be seriously flawed; indeed, the situation is often the opposite of what its proponents understand it to be. Racist speech, far from serving as a pressure valve, deepens minorities' predicament. Except in authoritarian countries like South Africa, authorities generally do not apply antiracism rules against minorities. Free speech has not generally proven a trusty friend of racial reformers. And talking back is rarely a realistic possibility for the victim of hate speech.

THE PRESSURE VALVE ARGUMENT

The pressure valve argument holds that rules prohibiting hate speech are unwise because they increase minorities' vulnerability. Forcing racists to bottle up their dislike of minority group members means that they will be likely to say or do something more hurtful later. Free speech functions like a pressure valve, allowing tension to dissipate before it reaches a dangerous level. The argument is paternalistic in that it says, we need to deny you what you say you want, for your own good; antiracism rules will really make matters worse; if you understood this, you would join us in opposing them.

Hate speech may make the speaker feel better, at least momentarily, but it does not make the victim safer. Quite the contrary. Social science evidence shows that permitting one person to say or do hateful things to another *increases*, rather than decreases, the likelihood that he or she will do so in the future.

POLITICAL CORRECTNESS AND HATE SPEECH

The role of harassment and intimidation in the maintenance of subordination is both historical and enduring. While foes of political correctness charge the imposition of orthodoxy, their efforts support the survival of an orthodoxy far more troubling—that racial harassment is both ordinary and privileged. There is much room for debate over the appropriateness of particular measures. But the argument that restraint of racial harassment is impermissible is the equivalent of the untenable proposition that individuals must accept rights—housing, education, employment—under subordinating conditions. The charge that measures to provide more than token equality impose political correctness obscures the equality dimension of racial hate speech. The censorship charge cloaks permissiveness on racism in a lovely philosophical garment. The time has come to strip it away and look directly at the ugliness it conceals and protects.

Linda S. Greene, *National Forum*, Spring 1995.

Moreover, this permission will lead others to believe that they may follow suit. Human beings are not mechanical objects; our behavior is more complex than the laws of physics that describe pressure valves, tanks, or the behavior of a gas in a tube. In particular, we use symbols to construct our social world, one that contains categories and expectations for "black," "woman," "child," "criminal," "wartime enemy," and so on. The roles we create for each other, once in place, govern the way we speak of and act toward each other in the future. . . .

Allowing individuals to revile others, then, does not render the others safer, but more at risk. Once the speaker identifies someone as being in the category of deserved victim, his or her behavior toward that person is likely to escalate from reviling to bullying and physical violence. Further, social science literature shows that stereotypical treatment tends to generalize: what we do teaches others that they may do likewise. Pressure valves may make steam pipes safer; they don't work that way with human beings.

THE "REVERSE ENFORCEMENT" ARGUMENT

A reverse enforcement argument asserts that enacting antiracism rules is sure to hurt minorities because the new rules will eventually be applied against them. A vicious insult hurled by a white to a black will go unpunished, but even a mild expression of irritation by a black motorist to a police officer or a student to a professor will bring harsh sanctions. The argument gains plausibility because certain authorities are, indeed, racist and dislike blacks who speak out of turn, and because a few incidents of blacks charged with hate speech for innocuous behavior have occurred.

But the evidence does not suggest that this is the pattern, much less the rule. Police reports and FBI compilations show that hate crimes are committed much more frequently by whites against blacks than the reverse; statistics published by the National Institute Against Violence and Prejudice show the same patterns for hate speech. And the distribution of enforcement seems to be in keeping with that of the offenses. Although an occasional minority group member may, indeed, be charged with a hate crime or with violating a campus hate-speech code, such prosecutions are relatively rare. Racism, of course, is not a one-way street; some blacks, Latinos, and other minorities have harassed and badgered whites or one another. Still, the reverse enforcement objection seems to have little validity in the U.S. While a recent study of the international aspects of hate speech regulation showed that in repressive societies, such as South Africa and the former Soviet Union, laws against hate speech indeed have been applied to stifle dissenters and members of minority groups, this has not happened in more progressive countries. The likelihood that officials here would turn hate-speech laws into weapons against minorities seems remote.

FREE SPEECH AS MINORITIES' BEST FRIEND

Many First Amendment absolutists argue that this amendment historically has been a great friend and ally of reformers. Nadine Strossen, for example, argues that without free speech, Martin Luther King could not have moved the American public as he did. Other reform movements also are said to have relied heavily on speeches, exhortation, and appeals to conscience. This argument, like the two earlier ones, is paternalistic because it is based on a presumed best interest of the protected group: if that group understood where its welfare truly lay, the argument goes, it would not demand to bridle speech.

This argument rests on questionable historical premises; moreover, it misconceives the situation that exists today. Historically, minorities have made the greatest progress when they acted in *defiance* of the First Amendment. The original Constitution protected slavery in several of its provisions; for nearly one hundred years the First Amendment existed side by side with slavery. Free speech for slaves, women, and the propertyless was not a serious concern for the drafters of the amendment, who appear to have conceived it mainly as a protection for the type of refined political, scientific, and artistic discourse they and their class held dear.

Later, of course, abolitionism and civil rights activism broke out. But examination of the role of speech in these movements shows that the relationship of the First Amendment to social advance is not so simple as free-speech absolutists maintain. In the civil rights era, for example, Martin Luther King and others did use speech and other symbolic acts to appeal to America's conscience, but, as often as not, they found the First Amendment, as then understood, deployed *against* them. They rallied, but were arrested and convicted; sat in, but were arrested and convicted; marched, sang, and spoke—but were arrested and convicted. Their speech struck lawgivers as too forceful, too disruptive. Some years later, to be sure, some of their convictions would be reversed on appeal—at the cost of thousands of dollars and much gallant lawyering. But the First Amendment, as then understood, served more as an obstacle than a friend.

Maintaining the Status Quo

Why does this happen? Narrative theory shows that we interpret new stories in terms of old ones we have internalized and now use to judge reality, new stories that would recharacterize that reality not excepted. Stories that deviate too drastically from those that constitute our current understanding we denounce as false and dangerous. The free market of ideas is useful mainly for solving small, clearly bounded disputes. History shows it has proven much less useful for redressing deeply inscribed systemic evils, such as racism. Language requires an interpretive paradigm, a set of meanings that a group agrees to attach to words and terms. But if racism is a central paradigm—woven into a thousand scripts, stories, and roles—one cannot speak out against it without seeming incoherent or irresponsible.

An examination of the current landscape of First Amendment

doctrine reveals a similar pattern. Our system has carved out and now tolerates dozens of "exceptions" to the free speech principle—words of threat, conspiracy, or libel; copyrighted terms; misleading advertising; disrespectful words uttered to a judge, teacher, or other authority figure; plagiarism; and official secrets, to name a few. These exceptions (each responding to some interest of a powerful group) seem familiar and acceptable, as indeed perhaps they are. But the suggestion that we recognize a new one to protect some of the most defenseless members of society—for example, eighteen-year-old black undergraduates at predominantly white campuses—immediately produces consternation. Suddenly the First Amendment must be a seamless web.

This language is ironic, however, for it is we who are caught in a web, the web of the familiar. An instrument that seems to us valuable—that reflects our interests and sense of the world, that makes certain distinctions, that tolerates certain exceptions, that functions in a particular way—we assume will be equally valuable for others. But the First Amendment's history, as well as the current landscape of exceptions and special doctrines, shows it is far more valuable to the majority than to the minority; far more useful for maintaining the status quo than facilitating change.

"More Speech"

Some defenders of the First Amendment argue that minorities should simply talk back to their aggressors. Nat Hentoff writes that antiracism rules teach black people to depend on whites for protection, while talking back clears the air and strengthens one's self-image as an active agent in charge of one's own destiny. Talking back draws force from the First Amendment doctrine of "more speech," according to which additional dialogue is always a preferred response to speech that some find troubling. Proponents of this approach oppose antiracism rules not so much because the rules limit speech, but because they believe that it is good for minorities to learn to speak out. A few also argue that a minority who speaks out will be able to educate a speaker who has uttered a hurtful remark, to alter that speaker's perception by explaining matters, so that the speaker will no longer say such things in the future.

How valid is this argument? Like many paternalistic arguments, it is offered blandly, virtually as an article of faith. Those who make it are in a position of power (that is the nature of paternalism) and so believe themselves able to make things so merely by stating them. They rarely offer empirical proof of their claims because none is needed. The social world is as they say, because it is the world they created.

The "speak up" argument is similar to the "more speech" argument, and as weak. Those who hurl racial epithets do so because they feel empowered to utter them. One who talks back is seen as issuing a direct challenge to that power. Many racist remarks are delivered by a crowd to an individual, a situation in which responding in kind would be foolhardy. Many highly publicized cases of racial assault began in just this fashion: a group began badgering a black person; the victim talked back, and paid with his or her life. Other racist remarks are delivered in a cowardly fashion, by means of graffiti scrawled on a campus wall late at night or a leaflet placed under a student's dormitory door. In these situations, talking back, of course, is impossible.

HATE SPEECH DENIES EQUALITY

Education today is the linchpin of equality, just as it is the key determinant of meaningful social and economic opportunity in the United States. Therefore, the mission of the university must include the right, as well as the responsibility, to guarantee students and faculty of color unfettered and equitable access to the full educational and pedagogical enterprise. The purpose of hate speech in this context is not to expand discourse, but to deprive targeted group members of their civil and educational rights. Tolerance of hate-speech activities in this setting contradicts our fundamental notions of justice and equality.

Robin D. Barnes, *The Price We Pay: The Case Against Racist Speech, Hate Propaganda, and Pornography*, ed. Laura J. Lederer and Richard Delgado, 1995.

Racist speech is rarely a mistake, rarely something that could be corrected or countered by discussion. What would be the answer to "Nigger, go back to Africa. You don't belong here"? "Sir, you misconceive the situation. Prevailing ethics and constitutional interpretation hold that I, an African American, am an individual of equal dignity and entitled to attend this university in the same manner as others. Now that you understand this, I am sure you will modify your remarks in the future"? The idea that talking back is safe for the black person or potentially educative for the white person is a dangerous fiction. It ignores the power dimension to racist remarks, encourages minorities to run very real risks, and treats as an invitation to dialogue that which has the opposite intent—the banishment of the victim from the human community. Even when successful, talking back is a burden. Why should minority undergraduates, already charged with their own education, be responsible for educating others?

HUBRIS

In summary, the four paternalistic arguments do not bear close analysis. Powerful and well-connected whites who resist hate-speech rules must realize that the reasons for that resistance lie on their side of the ledger. Censorship and governmental nest-feathering are not concerns when speech is private. Nor does targeted racial vilification promote any of the theoretical rationales for protecting free speech, such as facilitation of political discourse or self-fulfillment of the speaker. Much less does toleration of racist name-calling benefit the victim, as the American Civil Liberties Union (ACLU) and others have argued. Far from acting as a pressure valve that enables rage to dissipate harmlessly, epithets increase their victims' vulnerability. Demeaning images create a world in which some are one down, and others come to see them as legitimate victims. . . . They are targeted for mistreatment. This mistreatment ranges from slights and derision to denial of jobs and even beatings.

The Greeks had another term for this paternalism: *hubris*, defined by Kenneth J. Dover as the crime of believing that one may "treat other people just as one pleases, with the arrogant confidence that one will escape any penalty for violating their rights." Those who tell ethnic jokes and hurl epithets are guilty of this kind of arrogance. But those who defend these practices, including some backers of First Amendment absolutism, are guilty as well. Insisting on free speech above all, as though *no* countervailing interests were at stake; putting forward transparently paternalistic justifications for a regime in which hate speech is as protected as political discourse—these are also *hubris*, the insistence of someone powerful that what he or she values must also be what you want. Unilateral power is prone to this kind of arrogance, this insistence that one person's worldview, interests, way of framing an issue, is the only one.

Unfettered speech, a free market in which only some prevail, becomes an exercise in power. Insistence that this current regime is necessary and virtuous, that minorities acquiesce in a definition of virtue that condemns them to second-class status, and that their refusal to do so is evidence of their childlike simplicity and incomprehension of their own condition—this may well be the greatest hubris of all.

"The First Amendment to the United States Constitution protects speech no matter how offensive its content."

HATE SPEECH SHOULD NOT BE RESTRICTED

American Civil Liberties Union

The American Civil Liberties Union (ACLU) is a national organization that works to defend civil rights guaranteed by the U.S. Constitution. In the following viewpoint, the ACLU argues that hate speech is protected by the First Amendment and therefore cannot be restricted. Codes that prohibit hate speech on college campuses do not solve the problem of bigotry, the organization contends; instead, such codes simply drive bigotry underground where it is more difficult to combat. According to the ACLU, the best way to combat hate speech is through education and a tolerant environment.

As you read, consider the following questions:
1. In the ACLU's opinion, why should hate speech be kept out in the open?
2. When should speech be considered conduct, and therefore no longer protected by the First Amendment, according to the ACLU?
3. What specific measures should college administrators employ to combat hate speech on campus, according to the ACLU?

Reprinted from "Hate Speech on Campus," *ACLU Briefing Paper*, no. 16 (1996), by permission of the American Civil Liberties Union.

In recent years, a rise in verbal abuse and violence directed at people of color, lesbians and gay men, and other historically persecuted groups has plagued the United States. Among the settings of these expressions of intolerance are college and university campuses, where bias incidents have occurred sporadically since the mid-1980s. Outrage, indignation and demands for change have greeted such incidents—understandably, given the lack of racial and social diversity among students, faculty and administrators on most campuses.

Many universities, under pressure to respond to the concerns of those who are the objects of hate, have adopted codes or policies prohibiting speech that offends any group based on race, gender, ethnicity, religion or sexual orientation.

THE WRONG RESPONSE

That's the wrong response, well-meaning or not. The First Amendment to the United States Constitution protects speech no matter how offensive its content. Speech codes adopted by government-financed state colleges and universities amount to government censorship, in violation of the Constitution. And the American Civil Liberties Union (ACLU) believes that all campuses should adhere to First Amendment principles because academic freedom is a bedrock of education in a free society.

How much we value the right of free speech is put to its severest test when the speaker is someone we disagree with most. Speech that deeply offends our morality or is hostile to our way of life warrants the same constitutional protection as other speech because the right of free speech is indivisible: When one of us is denied this right, all of us are denied. Since its founding in 1920, the ACLU has fought for the free expression of all ideas, popular or unpopular. That's the constitutional mandate.

Where racist, sexist and homophobic speech is concerned, the ACLU believes that more speech—not less—is the best revenge. This is particularly true at universities, whose mission is to facilitate learning through open debate and study, and to enlighten. Speech codes are not the way to go on campuses, where all views are entitled to be heard, explored, supported or refuted. Besides, when hate is out in the open, people can see the problem. Then they can organize effectively to counter bad attitudes, possibly change them, and forge solidarity against the forces of intolerance.

College administrators may find speech codes attractive as a quick fix, but as one critic put it: "Verbal purity is not social change." Codes that punish bigoted speech treat only the symptom: The problem itself is bigotry. The ACLU believes that instead of opting for gestures that only appear to cure the disease, universities have to do the hard work of recruitment to increase faculty and student diversity, counseling to raise awareness about bigotry and its history, and changing curricula to institutionalize more inclusive approaches to all subject matter.

QUESTIONS AND ANSWERS ABOUT HATE SPEECH

Question: I just can't understand why the ACLU defends free speech for racists, sexists, homophobes and other bigots. Why tolerate the promotion of intolerance?

Answer: Free speech rights are indivisible. Restricting the speech of one group or individual jeopardizes everyone's rights because the same laws or regulations used to silence bigots can be used to silence you. Conversely, laws that defend free speech for bigots can be used to defend the rights of civil rights workers, anti-war protesters, lesbian and gay activists and others fighting for justice. For example, in the 1949 case of *Terminiello v. Chicago*, the ACLU successfully defended an ex–Catholic priest who had delivered a racist and anti-semitic speech. The precedent set in that case became the basis for the ACLU's successful defense of civil rights demonstrators in the 1960s and '70s.

The indivisibility principle was also illustrated in the case of Neo-Nazis whose right to march in Skokie, Illinois in 1979 was successfully defended by the ACLU. At the time, then ACLU Executive Director Aryeh Neier, whose relatives died in Hitler's concentration camps during World War II, commented: "Keeping a few Nazis off the streets of Skokie will serve Jews poorly if it means that the freedoms to speak, publish or assemble any place in the United States are thereby weakened."

Q: I have the impression that the ACLU spends more time and money defending the rights of bigots than supporting the victims of bigotry!!??

A: Not so. Only a handful of the several thousand cases litigated by the national ACLU and its affiliates every year involves offensive speech. Most of the litigation, advocacy and public education work we do preserves or advances the constitutional rights of ordinary people. But it's important to understand that the fraction of our work that does involve people who've engaged in bigoted and hurtful speech is very important.

Defending First Amendment rights for the enemies of civil liberties and civil rights means defending it for you and me.

"FIGHTING WORDS"

Q: Aren't some kinds of communication not protected under the First Amendment, like "fighting words"?

A: The U.S. Supreme Court did rule in 1942, in a case called *Chaplinsky v. New Hampshire*, that intimidating speech directed at a specific individual in a face-to-face confrontation amounts to "fighting words," and that the person engaging in such speech can be punished if "by their very utterance [the words] inflict injury or tend to incite an immediate breach of the peace." Say a white student stops a black student on campus and utters a racial slur. In that one-on-one confrontation, which could easily come to blows, the offending student could be disciplined under the "fighting words" doctrine for racial harassment.

Dick Wright. Reprinted by permission of United Feature Syndicate, Inc.

Over the past 50 years, however, the Court hasn't found the "fighting words" doctrine applicable in any of the hate speech cases that have come before it, since the incidents involved didn't meet the narrow criteria stated above. Ignoring that history, the folks who advocate campus speech codes try to stretch the doctrine's application to fit words or symbols that cause discomfort, offense or emotional pain.

Q: *What about nonverbal symbols, like swastikas and burning crosses—are they constitutionally protected?*

A: Symbols of hate are constitutionally protected if they're worn or displayed before a general audience in a public place— say, in a march or at a rally in a public park. But the First Amendment doesn't protect the use of nonverbal symbols to encroach upon, or desecrate, private property, such as burning a cross on someone's lawn or spray-painting a swastika on the wall of a synagogue or dorm.

In its 1992 decision in *R.A.V. v. St. Paul*, the Supreme Court struck down as unconstitutional a city ordinance that prohibited cross-burnings based on their symbolism, which the ordinance said makes many people feel "anger, alarm or resentment." Instead of prosecuting the cross-burner for the content of his act, the city government could have rightfully tried him under criminal trespass and/or harassment laws.

The Supreme Court has ruled that symbolic expression, whether swastikas, burning crosses or, for that matter, peace signs, is protected by the First Amendment because it's "closely akin to 'pure speech.'" That phrase comes from a landmark 1969 decision in which the Court held that public school students could wear black armbands in school to protest the Vietnam War. And in another landmark ruling, in 1989, the Court upheld the right of an individual to burn the American flag in public as a symbolic expression of disagreement with government policies.

INEFFECTUAL AND COUNTER-PRODUCTIVE

Q: *Aren't speech codes on college campuses an effective way to combat bias against people of color, women and gays?*

A: Historically, defamation laws or codes have proven ineffective at best and counter-productive at worst. For one thing, depending on how they're interpreted and enforced, they can actually work against the interests of the people they were ostensibly created to protect. Why? Because the ultimate power to decide what speech is offensive and to whom rests with the authorities—the government or a college administration—not with those who are the alleged victims of hate speech.

In Great Britain, for example, a Racial Relations Act was adopted in 1965 to outlaw racist defamation. But throughout its existence, the Act has largely been used to persecute activists of color, trade unionists and anti-nuclear protesters, while the racists—often white members of Parliament—have gone unpunished.

Similarly, under a speech code in effect at the University of Michigan for 18 months, white students in 20 cases charged black students with offensive speech. One of the cases resulted in the punishment of a black student for using the term "white trash" in conversation with a white student. The code was struck down as unconstitutional in 1989 and, to date, the ACLU has brought successful legal challenges against speech codes at the Universities of Connecticut, Michigan and Wisconsin.

These examples demonstrate that speech codes don't really serve the interests of persecuted groups. The First Amendment does. As one African American educator observed: "I have always felt as a minority person that we have to protect the rights of all because if we infringe on the rights of any persons, we'll be next."

SPEECH CODES WILL NOT END BIGOTRY

Q: But don't speech codes send a strong message to campus bigots, telling them their views are unacceptable?

A: Bigoted speech is symptomatic of a huge problem in our country; it is not the problem itself. Everybody, when they come to college, brings with them the values, biases and assumptions they learned while growing up in society, so it's unrealistic to think that punishing speech is going to rid campuses of the attitudes that gave rise to the speech in the first place. Banning bigoted speech won't end bigotry, even if it might chill some of the crudest expressions. The mindset that produced the speech lives on and may even reassert itself in more virulent forms.

Speech codes, by simply deterring students from saying out loud what they will continue to think in private, merely drive biases underground where they can't be addressed. In 1990, when Brown University expelled a student for shouting racist epithets one night on the campus, the institution accomplished nothing in the way of exposing the bankruptcy of racist ideas.

SPEECH AND CONDUCT

Q: Does the ACLU make a distinction between speech and conduct?

A: Yes. The ACLU believes that hate speech stops being just speech and becomes conduct when it targets a particular individual, and when it forms a pattern of behavior that interferes with a student's ability to exercise his or her right to participate fully in the life of the university.

The ACLU isn't opposed to regulations that penalize acts of violence, harassment or intimidation, and invasions of privacy. On the contrary, we believe that kind of conduct should be punished. Furthermore, the ACLU recognizes that the mere presence of speech as one element in an act of violence, harassment, intimidation or privacy invasion doesn't immunize that act from punishment. For example, threatening, bias-inspired phone calls to a student's dorm room, or white students shouting racist epithets at a woman of color as they follow her across campus—these are clearly punishable acts.

Several universities have initiated policies that both support free speech and counter discriminatory conduct. Arizona State, for example, formed a "Campus Environment Team" that acts as an education, information and referral service. The team of specially trained faculty, students and administrators works to foster an environment in which discriminatory harassment is less likely to occur, while also safeguarding academic freedom and freedom of speech.

AN ATTEMPT TO DESTROY DISSENT

Hate-speech laws represent the attempt of the modern state to destroy dissent, and the reckless support for these efforts coming from various spokesmen for "victims" makes the battle for liberty even harder to wage. Take notice that the crusade against intellectual tolerance being packaged as a war against hate is not the work of isolated communities upholding tradition. It is the project of a modern, centralized state seeking to reconstruct human behavior and suppress unwelcome thought. One should think twice before picking this side as the side of reason and kindness.

Paul Gottfried, Insight, June 24, 1996.

Q:Well, given that speech codes are a threat to the First Amendment, and given the importance of equal opportunity in education, what type of campus policy on hate speech would the ACLU support?

A: The ACLU believes that the best way to combat hate speech on campus is through an educational approach that includes counter-speech, workshops on bigotry and its role in American and world history, and real—not superficial—institutional change.

Universities are obligated to create an environment that fosters tolerance and mutual respect among members of the campus community, an environment in which all students can exercise their right to participate fully in campus life without being discriminated against. Campus administrators on the highest level should, therefore,

- speak out loudly and clearly against expressions of racist, sexist, homophobic and other bias, and react promptly and firmly to acts of discriminatory harassment;
- create forums and workshops to raise awareness and promote dialogue on issues of race, sex and sexual orientation;
- intensify their efforts to recruit members of racial minorities on student, faculty and administrative levels;
- and reform their institutions' curricula to reflect the diversity of peoples and cultures that have contributed to human

knowledge and society, in the United States and throughout the world.

ACLU Executive Director Ira Glasser stated, in a speech at the City College of New York: "There is no clash between the constitutional right of free speech and equality. Both are crucial to society. Universities ought to stop restricting speech and start teaching."

"Some very minimal parameters on
the content even of political speech
will not suppress and may actually
be a condition of its continued
robustness."

FLAG BURNING AS POLITICAL SPEECH
SHOULD BE RESTRICTED

Richard Parker

In 1989 and 1990, the U.S. Supreme Court declared that two
laws prohibiting flag burning were unconstitutional because
they violated the right to free speech. Every year since then,
Congress has unsuccessfully attempted to pass a constitutional
amendment banning flag desecration. In the following viewpoint, Richard Parker supports the amendment. The flag is a
symbol of the country's national sovereignty, he asserts; desecrating it destroys that image. In addition, he maintains that
banning flag burning would not violate any rules against regulating the content of speech because no such rules exist. Parker
is a law professor at Harvard University and the author of *Here,
the People Rule: A Constitutional Manifesto.*

As you read, consider the following questions:
1. What, according to Parker, do flag amendment opponents say
   the flag symbolizes?
2. Why is the number of flag burnings irrelevant to the issue of
   enacting an amendment to protect the flag, according to the
   author?
3. How will people who use items adorned with flags be
   protected from charges of flag desecration, in Parker's
   opinion?

Reprinted from Richard Parker, "Old Glories in Tandem: Flag and Constitution," *The
Weekly Standard*, November 13, 1995, by permission of *The Weekly Standard.*

Forgotten the flag amendment? You shouldn't. . . . As a gauge of populist democracy, few current controversies are more telling than [an] amendment authorizing the people's representatives, if they choose, to "prohibit the physical desecration of the flag of the United States."

Since 1989, when a 5-4 majority on the Supreme Court first invalidated long taken-for-granted laws against flag desecration, most polls have shown decisive support for a flag amendment, often near 80 percent. At the same time, "thoughtful" commentators, unelected "opinion leaders," and, especially, the mainstream media have overwhelmingly opposed it. . . . Their reaction has been relentless and—in day-to-day "reporting," editorials, and op-ed pieces—relentlessly one-sided. Not just one-sided, but haughty, nasty, and often hysterical.

FORMULAIC ARGUMENTS

The arguments against the amendment have, also, been remarkably formulaic. The editorials, the op-ed pieces, and the "reporting" have knocked off the same claims again and again. Let's review the three main clusters of arguments. From the flagrancy of each, there spring—like flowers in a landfill—populist arguments in favor of the amendment. Taken together, they establish this issue as an index of the populist challenge to both establishment liberalism and establishment conservatism.

The flag is the unique symbol of our aspiration to national unity: That much is accepted by everyone as a starting point. What's contested, at the outset, is whether protection of this symbol should be taken seriously—along with subsidiary questions of whether protection is needed and whether it would be effective. Of course, the opponents say they "revere" the flag. Yet they belittle, even mock, the amendment on all these counts.

Here's how their argument goes. The flag, they say, is a "mere" symbol. They insist on boiling down its meaning. What it "really" stands for, they tell us, is a national commitment to certain official institutions, certain liberties under law. And the freedom the flag symbolizes, they go on, includes a freedom to burn it. They grant that flag desecration is "offensive." They compare it, however, to displays of Nazi or Klan regalia. The offensiveness of these displays to minority groups, they say, is no less—in fact, they suggest, it is greater. Hence, the freedom to offend such groups, they claim, dictates a freedom to burn the flag, which offends other groups. They conclude with a one-two punch: This freedom, they say, is pretty much without cost since the tendency to exercise it is, at the moment, weak. (There have been rather few flag burnings in the last several years.) They predict, on the other hand, that any attempt to restrict this freedom would be ineffective (hence costly) since the desire to exercise it is so strong and would only get stronger in the face of legal prohibition.

WHAT THE FLAG REPRESENTS

Take, first, the matter of what the flag symbolizes. We are, by now, accustomed to being told, by smug elites, what are the "real" issues in an election and what is the "real" meaning of this or that common experience. In this case, the meaning said to be the "real" one is especially revealing. Here we have many members of our self-imagined governing class identifying the flag with official concepts and processes for whose definition and operation they are in the habit of claiming primary, almost proprietary, responsibility. Thus Charles Fried—a former solicitor general who specializes in constitutional law—proclaims that the "thing itself," which the flag symbolizes, is the Constitution. How convenient. It's no surprise, then, that opponents of the amendment go on, with stunning circularity, to announce— as if we must, of course, take their word for it—that what the flag stands for is the freedom to burn it.

No less revealing is their comparison of the "offensiveness" of flag desecration to that of expression that's hurtful to certain minority groups. They insist on reducing everything—including the unique symbol of our aspiration to national unity—to competing interests of diverse groups. You can't help wondering why they are trying to obscure other values symbolized by the flag, values on a different, deeper dimension.

These, of course, involve aspirational bonds, not divisions, among Americans. They have to do with Americans *as a people*. They're about the nation, not the government. Even more, they're about a people—"We, the People"—that is supposed to govern itself. For ours is a nation defined not by any shared ethnicity, but by a political practice, a practice of popular sovereignty based in political equality. These are foundational values. They underlie official institutions. They undergird law. They precede the Constitution. And, as such, they threaten the pretensions of any elite.

THE FLAG AS A SYMBOL

When opponents of the amendment argue that protection of the flag is not needed and would be ineffective anyway, they reveal their bias yet again. Seeing themselves as responsible for good government—nowadays, they prefer to say "governance"—of the people, they take for granted that the problem is one of behavior control. But the number of flag burnings last year or next year is not what should most concern us. We're talking about a symbol here. Whether two or two hundred burnings of a flag damage the flag, as a symbol, depends on our *response* to the behavior. Don't forget why the amendment was proposed in the first place. When the court, in 1989, overturned the laws against flag desecration, it declared permissible what had long been understood to be impermissible. It officially demoted the unique symbol of our popular sovereignty to the level of myriad competing values and interests. Symbolically, it demoted the nation to the level of the government. Or, one might as well say, it turned the government, symbolically, against the nation. This at a moment when millions are convinced that the government has been doing just that for some time in all sorts of ways. This symbolic challenge by the court, in the name of the Constitution, is properly answered in the Constitution, by exercising the sovereign right of the people—symbolized by the flag—to amend it.

Too Much to Ask

It isn't the *idea* of desecrating the flag that the American people propose to ban. Any street-corner orator who takes a notion to should be able to stand on a soapbox and bad-mouth the American flag all day long—and apple pie and motherhood, too, if that's the way the speaker feels. It's a free country.

It's actually burning Old Glory, it's defacing the Stars and Stripes, it's the physical desecration of the flag of the United States that ought to be against the law. . . .

To turn aside when the American flag is defaced, with all that the flag means—yes, all that it *symbolizes*—is to ask too much of Americans.

Paul Greenberg, *San Diego Union-Tribune,* July 9, 1995.

So, we come back to the flag as a "mere" symbol. The argument denigrating it on this ground sits oddly in our era of identity politics. But, be that as it may, the thing to remember is that—views of the current legal establishment to the contrary notwithstanding—the Constitution is, above all, a symbolic document. Its genius is its grand ambiguity on crucial matters. It is not a set of rules and regulations. Nor is it a blueprint. Being in large part symbolic, it is hortatory. As such, it has helped summon astonishing political energy and creativity. And its boldest symbolic stroke was its first three words. Thus, in an era when our governing elites depreciate the ideal of popular sovereignty, the flag amendment simply seeks to reaffirm the exhortation of the framers.

THE FREEDOM OF SPEECH ISSUE

Turn now to the second cluster of arguments about the amendment. It has to do with freedom of speech. Libertarians—liberal and conservative—deplore the flag amendment as "mutilating" and even "desecrating" our most precious civil liberty. To undo the court's flag-burning decisions, they say, would violate an inviolable rule that forbids regulating the content of political expression. And, they insist, it would set down a subversive counterrule, which would authorize censorship, compel affirmation of political orthodoxy, and push toward totalitarianism. Only totalitarian governments, they claim, protect their flags. (Was the United States totalitarian until 1989?) Rising to a crescendo, they cry that we must never, ever "amend the First Amendment."

It surprises them that supporters of the flag amendment agree with most of the values and principles they invoke. I, for one, am a civil libertarian. I believe that, in a democracy, freedom of speech must be "robust and wide open." In fact, I think it ought to be more robust and wide open than it is now. For populists, public expression by all sorts of people—not just the "thoughtful" ones—is vital to popular sovereignty. Hence, unruly expressive "conduct" mustn't be sharply segregated from more genteel "speech." (Chief Justice William Rehnquist did that in dissent in the flag-burning cases.) Nor should "inarticulate" expression be devalued. (Rehnquist did that, too.) And it's because of these beliefs that many of us support the flag amendment. How could that be? Such a view doesn't show up on the radar screen of the establishment. The reason is that its screen is a mirror.

In the mirror, establishment libertarians see only themselves and their imagined opposites, oppressive and benighted. That's why they're so given to hyperbole. Thus, what blinds them to the populist position is a compulsion to exaggerate both the amendment's "contradiction" of current free speech principle and its likely effects. As people who deplore those who "play on fear," they can't seem to help doing it.

SPEECH CAN BE RESTRICTED

Consider the supposed "rule" against restriction of speech content. There is, of course, no such "rule." (Think of obscenity.)

There's no such "rule" even for political speech. The court has held that statements criticizing official conduct of a public official may be restricted, if they are known to be false and damage the reputation of the official. This was made clear by the Warren court—in an opinion by Justice William Brennan, the very opinion that celebrated freedom of speech as "robust and wide-open." It's been reaffirmed ever since. The idea must be this: Some very minimal parameters on the content even of political speech will not suppress and may actually be a condition of its continued robustness. Wide-open debate explodes and dies, after all, if there are absolutely no limits on what anyone says about anyone else.

On the right, on the left, and in the center, nowadays, it's widely agreed that these parameters have broken down and must be restored. On the right, it's thought that "uncivil" and "unreasoned" speech content needs to be checked. (The court, on occasion, has interpreted the First Amendment in light of that belief.) On the left, it's thought that "hate" speech, beyond face-to-face "fighting words," needs to be checked. (On occasion, the court has read the First Amendment in light of that belief as well.) The problem is that these prescriptions invite regulation so broad and vague that robust expression really might be suffocated. In the center, by contrast, there's support for *much more minimal* restraint—on intentional, physical trashing of the unique symbol of the bonds that *make wide-open debate possible.* This leaves it to individuals, in a thousand other ways, to criticize the government and even the aspiration to national unity, if they want. It simply affirms that there is some commitment to others, beyond mere obedience to the formal rule of law, that should be respected as a basis of a flourishing freedom of speech.

To picture what is at stake here, recall the civil rights movement. Recall not only its invocation of national ideals, but also its evocation of nationhood. Recall the famous photo of the Selma marchers carrying American flags. The question is: Will the next Martin Luther King have available to him or her a basic means of identification with the rest of us—an inclusive appeal to the bonds that, at least in aspiration, make us one?

MISREPRESENTATION

This is no subversion of free speech. Quite the opposite. To claim it is, opponents of the amendment have to misrepresent it. They can do so confident that no one will question them in the mainstream media. One example: In the *Washington Post*, Nat Hentoff equated prohibiting physical desecration of the flag with something very different—a mandatory flag salute, long ago held unconstitutional as a "compulsory rite," coercing a declaration of belief. Surely, he saw the difference. But, after a few paragraphs, he was back suggesting that advocates of the amendment want to make it a crime to "imagine" burning the flag. Is it too much to ask Hentoff and the others a version of the question asked by Joseph Welch: Have you no shame?

Since shame won't be forthcoming, here's another question. What is it they are afraid of? Playing their own game, I'd say what's "really" going on is this: Seeing themselves as responsible for "enlightened" government, they fear the idea of the nation, the prospect of popular sovereignty, the empowerment of ordinary people. The amendment excites their fear not just because it dramatically reasserts the idea of the nation. It addresses, also, the popular basis of robust, wide-open debate. And, what's more, the very process of amending the Constitution stirs their ultimate nightmare, of ordinary people—"rude blue-collar types," in the words of one of my colleagues—remaking basic law. And that leads to the third cluster of arguments.

"Tinkering" with the Constitution

Probably, the argument that opponents make most often is this last one: We must not "tinker" or "fiddle" or "fool with" the Constitution, they say. (Even Colin Powell said this. It seems to come easily to "thoughtful" people who haven't thought much about the matter.) Notice the verbs they use to describe the process of constitutional amendment. Almost invariably, they're full of disdain, belittling, insulting. Such verbs are rarely used to describe judicial interpretations or lawyers' interpretations or academic interpretations of the Constitution. Nothing could be more revealing—of what motivates the opponents and what should spur on advocates of the flag amendment—than this choice of words. From this root disdain for democracy, they spin out a cluster of related routine arguments.

The Constitution, they say, is too "fragile" to be touched (at least by callused hands). They speak "learnedly" of its "delicate balance." These soundbites, of course, are numbingly familiar. Their very familiarity may numb us to their absurdity. For, far from proving fragile, the Constitution has proved, over two centuries and radical shifts in its accepted meaning, to have an extraordinary tensile strength, enduring by adapting—through reinterpretation and through amendment—to circumstances, changing and unforeseen. Just as John Marshall promised long ago.

Suspecting this argument may not be convincing, they move

to another where they can have some fun (which is to say, where they can give their disdain a humorous free rein). Constitutional amendments, they—correctly—observe, may have unintended consequences. What they go on to claim—incorrectly—is that amendments will have specific, outrageous sorts of consequences, not intended by their drafters. So, they talk of (and flourish) all sorts of items with a flag logo on them: handkerchiefs, bathing suits, underwear, you name it. "These will count as flags!" they proclaim. Writing in *Time,* Barbara Ehrenreich focused—as most do, interestingly—on underwear. "[E]ven a small lapse of personal hygiene," she whooped, "may constitute a punishable offense."

Do these people have no faith at all in our court system? At one moment, they pose as traditionalist believers in the established system of "governance." Then, they imagine that judges, interpreting new—and very minimal—constitutional language, will go bonkers.

Amid the frivolity, the absurdity of their argument may, again, go unnoticed. Anyone who knows anything much about judges at the end of the twentieth century knows that they will be suspicious of new constitutional provisions. They will read them sensibly, even narrowly. They will look to the recorded intent of the framers. And they will harmonize them with older provisions. Hence, what counts as a "flag" and as "physical desecration" will be influenced (possibly determined) by the statute Congress enacts under the amendment and, in any event, will be tightly limited by common sense and the First Amendment.

Time to Take Up the Reins

And, so, the opponents are reduced to their last argument. The Constitution, they cry, is perfect as is. It is not "a rough draft," intones Representative Pat Schroeder. Here, the absurdity swells wonderfully and turns back on itself. For if the Constitution is perfect, part of its perfection must be Article V, which provides for its amendment.

What the framers called for in Article V is a democratic process through which the people—the nation—may pull the reins on the government, reins which the framers meant, always, to be in the hands of the sovereign people. In this century, the people's grip on the reins has slackened. Isn't it time—now—to take hold? To establish, again, the constitutional premise of self-rule? To confirm that we are, after all and above all, one nation?

"[A] flag desecration amendment would actually tarnish and diminish the flag by undermining the very freedoms and values for which it . . . stand[s]."

FLAG BURNING AS POLITICAL SPEECH SHOULD NOT BE RESTRICTED

Part I: Roger Pilon, Part II: Carole Shields

The following two-part viewpoint is taken from the congressional testimonies of Roger Pilon and Carole Shields before the House Judiciary Committee's Subcommittee on the Constitution concerning a proposed constitutional amendment to ban flag burning that was passed in the House on June 12, 1997. In Part I, Pilon argues that flag desecration is political speech, and as such, is protected under the First Amendment. In Part II, Shields agrees, maintaining that the best way to honor the freedom that the flag symbolizes is by permitting offensive political dissent. Pilon is a senior fellow at the Cato Institute, a libertarian public policy research organization, and director of the institute's Center for Constitutional Studies. Shields is the president of People For the American Way.

As you read, consider the following questions:

1. What is the difference between defending the right to desecrate the flag and defending flag desecration, in Pilon's opinion?
2. Why did the framers of the Constitution want to protect political expression, according to Pilon?
3. In Shields's opinion, what is the best way to honor the flag?

Reprinted from the testimonies of Roger Pilon and Carole Shields in H.J. Res. 54: Proposing an Amendment to the Constitution of the United States Authorizing Congress to Prohibit the Desecration of the Flag of the United States, hearing before the Subcommittee on the Constitution, Committee on the Judiciary, House of Representatives, 105th Cong., 1st sess., April 30, 1997.

I

Let me . . . mak[e] clear from the outset what should be beyond any doubt, namely, that I am not here to defend those who would desecrate the flag of the United States. I dare say, in fact, that my contempt for such action is equal to that of any member of this subcommittee. For the flag is not simply the symbol of America; more deeply, it is the symbol of the principles on which this nation rests. Those who would desecrate the flag are thus guilty, at bottom, of desecrating our principles, which is why we find their acts so offensive. Ironically, however, it is those very principles that protect such acts—and restrain the rest of us in the process.

In a word, therefore, I am here not to defend flag desecration but to defend the right to desecrate the flag, offensive as the exercise of that right may be to so many Americans. That position may strike some as contradictory. It is not. In fact, there is all the difference in the world between defending the right to desecrate the flag and defending flag desecration itself. It is the difference between a free and an unfree society. This amendment, as it tries to shield us from offensive behavior, gives rise to even greater offense. By offending our very principles, it undermines its essential purpose, making us all less free.

POLITICAL SPEECH IS PROTECTED

Let me plumb those issues a bit more deeply by noting, first, that flag desecration of a kind that this amendment would authorize Congress to prohibit is political expression and, second, that political expression is precisely what the Framers wanted most to protect when they drafted the First Amendment. In a pair of cases decided in 1989 and 1990—involving first a state, then a federal statute—the United States Supreme Court said as much, which is why those who want to prohibit people from engaging in such acts have resorted to a constitutional amendment—an amendment that would, for the first time in over 200 years, amend the First Amendment. That alone should give pause.

But it is not the First Amendment alone that protects the rights of political expression. Even before the Bill of Rights was ratified, two years after the Constitution itself was ratified, citizens were protected against overweening federal power by a simple yet profound expedient—the doctrine of enumerated powers. In a word, there was simply no power enumerated in the Constitution through which the federal government might abridge political expression. Arguing against the addition of a

Bill of Rights in Federalist 84, Alexander Hamilton put the point well: "Why declare that things shall not be done [by the federal government] which there is no power to do?" This amendment would expand federal power in a way the Framers plainly contemplated—and rejected.

PROTECTING THE RIGHTS OF SOCIETY'S LEAST POPULAR MEMBERS

It is crucial, however, to understand precisely why the Framers wanted to protect political expression. To be sure, they thought such expression was essential to the workings of a free society: democracy works, after all, only when people are free to participate in the processes through which they govern themselves. But it was not a concern for good consequences alone that drove the Framers: more deeply, they were concerned about the simple matter of protecting rights, whatever the consequences of doing so. The protection of our rights is tested, however, not when what we do or say is popular but when it is unpopular. Stated most starkly, a free society is tested by the way it protects the rights of its least popular members.

Sir Winston Churchill captured well that essential feature of our system when he observed in 1945 that "the United States is a land of free speech. Nowhere is speech freer—not even [in England], where we sedulously cultivate it even in its most repulsive forms." In so observing, Churchill was merely echoing thoughts attributed to Voltaire, that he may disapprove of what you say but would defend to the death your right to say it, and the ironic question of Benjamin Franklin: "Abuses of the freedom of speech ought to be repressed; but to whom are we to commit the power of doing it?"

THE PRINCIPLE OF THE MATTER

When so many for so long have understood the principles at issue today, how can this Congress so lightly abandon those principles? It is said by some that the flag is a special case, a unique symbol. That claim may be true, but it does not go to the principle of the matter: in a free society, individuals have a right to express themselves, even in offensive ways. Once we bar such expression, however, Franklin's question will immediately be upon us. What is more, we will soon find that the flag is not unique, that the Bible and much else will next be in line for special protection.

It is said also that the flag is special because men have fought and died for it. Let me suggest in response that men have fought and died not for the flag but for the principles it represents. People give their lives for principles, not for symbols. When we dishonor those principles, to protect their symbol, we dishonor the men who died to preserve them. That is not a business this Congress should be about. We owe it to those men, men who have made the ultimate sacrifice, to resist the pressures of the moment so that we may preserve the principles of the ages.

II

In an effort to solve a problem that does not exist, the proposed flag desecration amendment would actually tarnish and diminish the flag by undermining the very freedoms and values for which it and our constitutional republic so proudly stand. This is not the American Way.

PROTECTING AMERICAN VALUES

In 1980, a group of civic and religious leaders founded People For the American Way in order to combat intolerance and to affirm our common heritage and fundamental American values of "pluralism, individuality, freedom of thought, expression and religion, a sense of community, and tolerance and compassion for others." Since then, People For the American Way has worked hard to promote and protect these values and individual freedoms, whether it be in the area of religion, the arts, the public schools, the public libraries, or politics.

My own passion for these values comes directly from my religious upbringing in the South. My father, my grandfather, and two of my uncles were Southern Baptist preachers with a straightforward and powerful core theological belief in the individual's freedom of conscience. It is this deep and abiding religious and moral conviction in individual freedom that I bring to this issue, and that forms the bedrock for my unwillingness to sacrifice substance for symbolism where fundamental liberty is at stake. These are the values that brought me to People For the American Way. From its beginning, this organization has stood firmly against cynical attempts to use the American flag as a political wedge issue which would undermine the very liberties that make the United States the beacon of freedom for the rest of the world.

THE BILL OF RIGHTS HAS NEVER BEEN AMENDED

Though some today seem not to be aware of it, the Bill of Rights is not a first draft. For over two centuries, Congress has never, ever passed a constitutional amendment to restrict the Bill of Rights. That's a tribute to the wisdom of Congress—and the good sense of the American people who understand how fortunate we are to live in a nation whose Bill of Rights protects our most basic freedoms. That is why, according to a 1995 Peter Hart poll commissioned by the American Bar Association, a majority of Americans opposed a flag desecration amendment by 52% to 38% when they were informed that it would be the first in the nation's history to restrict First Amendment freedoms.

Reprinted by permission of Mike Luckovich and Creators Syndicate.

We can all well appreciate the strong feelings engendered by this issue. Destroying or disrespecting the American flag as part of a political protest is highly offensive. However, at the same time, it is undeniably a political statement and thus cuts to the core of the First Amendment. As the Supreme Court has properly held time and time again, it is a "bedrock principle underlying the First Amendment...that the Government may not prohibit the expression of an idea simply because society finds the idea itself offensive and disagreeable." Moreover, as Justice Robert Jackson eloquently stated over 50 years ago, "Freedom to differ is not limited to things that do not matter much. That would be a mere shadow of freedom. The test of its substance is the right to differ as to things that touch the heart of the existing order."

America is a strong enough country to tolerate political demonstrations—even extreme and offensive ones—and tell the demonstrators: "We disagree with every word you say, but we will defend unto death your right to say it." Indeed, to ban so-called flag desecration would put America in the unwelcome league of totalitarian states such as China and the former Soviet Union which fear dissent and oppose our freedoms of expression and peaceful assembly and protest. We ought not to allow a handful of offensive protesters to achieve what the fascists we fought in World War II and the communists we resisted during the Cold War could not—to make us surrender our most fundamental freedoms. We are a stronger nation and a stronger people than that.

NO FLAG-BURNING CRISIS

What is the urgent crisis then that impels the need to voluntarily surrender the freedoms in our Bill of Rights for the first time in our nation's history? Flag burning as part of a political protest, as opposed to the proper disposing of a worn flag, is an exceedingly rare occurrence in our country. Published reports indicate only a handful of such occurrences since the Supreme Court's flag decisions of 1989 and 1990. If anything, the historical evidence suggests that outlawing so-called "flag desecration" will only increase flag burnings and acts of disrespect for the flag by those who seek attention. Nor is there any evidence that the few flag burnings that have occurred have in any way diminished the patriotic feelings of Americans for the flag and their country. To the contrary, as Professor Robert Justin Goldstein points out in his excellent history of the American flag desecration controversy, public outrage at Gregory Lee Johnson's burning of the flag in Dallas in the early 1980's only increased the public's reverence for the flag and patriotic feeling. Unlike totalitarian states, Americans need not coerce patriotism. It is a much greater love of country that we enjoy, one that is born of free will and devotion.

Unfortunately, there are some who feel that they can garner political gains by using the flag as a wedge issue to question the patriotism of those who oppose the amendment. This divisive and cynical strategy disserves America and is itself an abuse of the flag. Indeed, ironically, as Professor Goldstein points out in his book, at the turn of the century, outrage at the use of the flag as part of partisan, political campaign ads was one of the driving forces behind the movement for flag protection legislation. Furthermore, the evidence suggests that this issue may not even achieve the hoped-for political gains. Public reports and analysis of the 1996 elections show that the six incumbent Senators targeted by supporters of the amendment were all reelected and that the flag issue either was a non-issue or backfired in these campaigns. As the recent elections demonstrate, the American public wants Congress to focus on the real issues affecting their daily lives and well being.

In conclusion, we honor the flag best by defending the fundamental constitutional freedoms and values for which it stands. This is truly the American Way.

"Pornography is not compatible with the civil liberties of women."

THE GOVERNMENT SHOULD LEGISLATE AGAINST PORNOGRAPHY

Catherine Itzin

Pornography is not about sexual expression, argues Catherine Itzin in the following viewpoint, but about the objectification and subordination of women and children. This treatment of women and children is harmful, she contends. Instead of censoring pornography, Itzin favors legislation that would allow victims of pornography to sue the manufacturers and distributors for the harm they have experienced. Itzin is an honorary research fellow in the Violence Abuse and Gender Relations Research Unit at the University of Bradford in Massachusetts. She is also the editor and coauthor of *Pornography: Women, Violence and Civil Liberties.*

As you read, consider the following questions:

1. What evidence does Itzin present to support her view that pornography is about power and sexual objectification?
2. In Itzin's opinion, what is the real free speech issue for women concerning pornography?
3. Why is censoring pornography not the answer, according to the author?

Reprinted from Catherine Itzin, "Pornography and Civil Liberties," *National Forum: Phi Kappa Phi Journal*, vol. 75, no. 2 (Spring 1995), © by Catherine Itzin, by permission of the publisher.

"I can't define pornography," said a U.S. Supreme Court judge, "but I know what it is when I see it." Indeed. Most people do. Pornography is an industry that manufactures and markets a very profitable product. The people who make it, sell it, buy it, and use it know exactly what it is. So why has the belief been fostered that it is somehow indefinable and that defining it for purposes of legislation would be difficult or impossible?

One of the main reasons is that pornography has traditionally been seen in terms of "morality." The laws against pornography were—and in the United States and the United Kingdom still are—"obscenity laws." And the definition of obscenity is vague, subjective, and reflects little more than the dominant mores and values of the day. Morality is, and always has been, anti-sex and even more so, anti-women.

Furthermore, art and literature have been censored by means of these laws. Homosexuality—whether lesbian or gay—has been, and still is, regarded as inherently obscene. In 1936, Radclyffe Hall's *The Well of Loneliness* was declared obscene because it dealt with lesbianism. Nearly fifty years later, in 1984, the London bookshop "Gay's the Word" was prosecuted and 800 items seized on the same grounds. Among the titles were works by Oscar Wilde, Kate Millet, and Jean Genet—books that would have merited no legal action had they been heterosexual.

OBSCENITY AND PORNOGRAPHY

The irony is that while obscenity legislation can lead to censorship of non-pornographic material, it poses no real threat to pornography itself. If anything, it protects pornography. Obscenity laws look to see whether men are or the moral fabric of society is "depraved and corrupted" (a concept that has been shown through case law to have no consistent or practicable meaning at all). The law does not look at pornography from the position of women and children. If it did, it would see that this is not an issue of morality but of power and of sexual objectification, sexual subordination, sexual violence, and eroticized inequality.

You do not have to look far to find the evidence. In the United Kingdom, the top shelves of newsstands in every neighborhood are stocked with mainstream so-called "adult entertainment" magazines containing photographs of women's vaginas and anuses, pulled open and posed gaping for the camera, inviting penetration: women presented as constantly sexually available, insatiable and voracious, or passive and servile, serving men sexually. There are forms of technically legal child pornography where women have their pubic hair shaved and are posed to look like little girls, linking male sexual arousal to children's bodies. There is also sexual violence, with women being humiliated, whipped, and beaten.

Illegal pornography also circulates, sold from under the counter. This pornography features women bound and gagged, raped and tortured: cigarette burns on their breasts and genitals, labia nailed to the top of a table, hanging by their breasts from meat hooks. It includes visual records of child sexual abuse (called child pornography) and material promoting pre-pubescent sex. There is evidence of the existence of "snuff films" in which women and children are sexually murdered on camera.

Obscenity legislation looks at this, and because it sees nakedness and genitals, and because it is sexually arousing, it just sees "sex." In the sexually explicit, sexualized context of pornography, the dehumanization and subordination of women in the so-called soft-core pornography and the violence and torture of women in the so-called hard-core pornography are not recognized as such. . . .

THE HARM IN MAKING PORNOGRAPHY

Apart from the harm that is visible in pornography . . . a very substantial body of evidence shows that women and children are harmed through the making and use of pornography.

If we look at the experience of women working within the pornography industry, we find chilling accounts of sexual violence, rape, and coercion. The case of Linda Marchiano—who under the name of Linda Lovelace was the "star" of the 1970s porn film Deep Throat—is one of many examples. Linda—presented in the film as "liberated" and with an insatiable appetite for fellatio—was held captive for two years under threat of death by her boss, Charles Traynor. During the filming, she was hypnotized to suppress the normal gag response. She was tortured when she tried to escape, was never let out of Traynor's sight, and at gunpoint, suffered innumerable other indignities. When she finally escaped and told her story, it was echoed by that of a great many other women involved in the pornography business.

During hearings held by Minneapolis City Council in 1983 when the Council was considering an ordinance to add pornography as discrimination against women to existing civil rights statutes, ex-prostitutes described being forced by their pimps to be filmed having sex with dogs, or by the "johns" to copy what they had seen in pornography: one had her pubic hair removed with a jackknife, another was tied to a chair by a group of men carrying S&M magazines who burnt her with cigarettes, attached metal clips to her breasts, and raped and beat her continuously for twelve hours. In the United Kingdom, a recent article in the *Guardian* describes the film of a ten-year-old boy with his wrists tied together at his throat and his feet tied to a hook above his head while a group of men penetrate him anally and orally with their fingers, fists, and penises. The boy is crying. The film sells for £50. This article also includes an interview with a woman who was used throughout her childhood for the making of pornographic films: with adults, animals, and other children. These examples illustrate some of the harm experienced by women and children in the making of pornography. . . .

PORNOGRAPHY AND THE LAW

Government inquiries in Canada (1985), the United States (1986), Australia (1988), and New Zealand (1989) have accepted the evidence of the links between pornography and harm to women and children. In 1992, the Canadian Supreme Court ruled unanimously that violent, subordinating, and dehumanizing pornography contributes to sexual violence and reinforces sexual inequality. The courts in Canada also have successfully used the three academic research categories and the evidence of harm to prosecute violent and subordinating material and to acquit sexually explicit material that is nonviolent and nonsubordinating (including gay and lesbian material).

Even the Federal court in the United States, which in 1985 considered the civil rights ordinance drafted by the lawyer Catharine MacKinnon and the writer Andrea Dworkin and which was passed by the Minneapolis and Indianapolis city councils, concluded that "pornography is a systematic practice of exploitation and subordination based on sex that differentially harms women. The bigotry and contempt it produces, the acts of aggression it fosters, harm women's opportunities for equality and rights of all kinds." But the Court then decided that "this simply demonstrated the power of pornography as speech" and ruled that the free speech rights of the pornography industry took precedence over women's rights to be free of sexual violence and inequality.

The real free speech issue for women is getting access to speech, and the free speech issue in current debates on pornography is being able to speak very much at all against pornography. Women who do speak against pornography are attacked constantly, stereotyped and monsterized, not just by the pornography industry, but also by the sexual liberals and the libertarian left, who include the defenders of sado-masochism and who define sexual liberation in terms of sexual violence and sadistic pornography.

Among the misrepresentations and distortions emanating from these constituencies are that feminist antipornography campaigners have made alliances with the religious right, are sexually repressed, and believe that pornography is the sole cause of women's oppression. This is all demonstrably untrue, as is the suggestion that being against pornography means being for censorship. On the contrary: given the scale of harm to which it contributes, it is clear that pornography is not compatible with the civil liberties of women.

LIMITING PORNOGRAPHY WITHOUT CENSORSHIP

So what is the answer? Should there be state censorship of violent and subordinating pornography? I do not think so. Censorship is dangerous: freedom of speech matters. And it is now possible to legislate against pornography without censorship, using a harm-based equality approach rather than the obscenity approach that has proven to be unenforceable, inappropriate, and ineffective in dealing with pornography and has been used to prosecute gay and lesbian material which is not pornography.

One proposal in the United Kingdom is for sex-discrimination legislation that would enable people who could prove they were victims of pornography-related harm to take civil action against the manufacturers and distributors of pornography. This would not ban the publication of pornography, and it would give no power to the state to censor.

PORNOGRAPHY DOES NOT DESERVE FREE-SPEECH PROTECTION

It is utter flimflammery to insist that we have to get social scientists to prove that, for instance, pornography does harm. Independently of any proof of harm that certain types of expression do, we can recognize these types as being at best worthless, and therefore not worth protecting. Any rational ground for thinking that they do some harm is sufficient for prohibiting them.

Francis Canavan, *Moral Ideas for America*, ed. Larry P. Arnn and Douglas A. Jeffrey, 1993.

Another proposal is to use the U.K. Race Relations Act as a model for legislating against pornography that could be shown to have contributed to the incitement of sexual hatred and violence. In the United Kingdom, race-hatred literature is illegal because of the "identifiable harm" it causes to Black and Jewish people who do not regard the legislation as censorship, but as a guarantee of a measure of some freedom from racial hatred, violence, and discrimination. Why should not the same thing apply to women and pornography?

Take pornography out of the moral realm and place it in the context of the evidence of harm and the structures of power and abuse, and you find that it is not impossible to define at all. MacKinnon and Dworkin came up with a workable legal definition at the request of the City Council of Minneapolis. Pornography, they say, is graphic, sexually explicit, and it subordinates women. It also presents women in one or more of the following eight conditions of harm:

- dehumanized as sexual objects, things, or commodities;
- as sexual objects who enjoy humiliation or pain;
- as sexual objects who experience sexual pleasure in rape, incest, or other sexual assault; as sexual objects tied up, cut up, or mutilated or bruised, or physically hurt;
- in positions and postures of sexual submission, servility, or display;
- being penetrated by objects or animals;
- in scenarios of degradation, humiliation, injury, and torture;
- shown as filthy or inferior, bleeding, bruised, or hurt in a context that makes these conditions sexual;
- with their body parts (including vaginas, breasts, buttocks, or anuses) exhibited such that women are reduced to those parts.

Although this definition is based upon the treatment of women, it also applies to children or men or transsexuals—and so it covers pedophilia and violent and subordinating gay pornography but excludes erotica.

None of this could guarantee the elimination of sexism and sexual violence any more than the abolition of slavery ended racism and racial violence. But like pornography today, Black slavery in the United States was a major international profit-making industry—and it was ended.

People have agreed to forgo certain freedoms because of the damage and harm they do to other people. In the United Kingdom, these include the freedom to steal, to assault, to rape, to murder, to incite racial hatred and discrimination, and to discriminate in employment on the grounds of race or sex.

The freedom to incite sexual hatred, sexual violence, and sex discrimination through pornography is another freedom people should agree to forgo to ensure and safeguard the freedom, safety, and civil liberties of women.

| "Make no mistake: if accepted, the feminist procensorship analysis would lead inevitably to the suppression of far more than pornography."

PORNOGRAPHY SHOULD NOT BE RESTRICTED

Nadine Strossen

In the following viewpoint, Nadine Strossen argues that the First Amendment contains no exception for sexual speech. If sexual speech is censored or regulated, she contends, then other forms of political expression will also be threatened. Strossen is the president of the American Civil Liberties Union and the author of *Defending Pornography: Free Speech, Sex, and the Fight for Women's Rights*, from which this viewpoint is excerpted.

As you read, consider the following questions:

1. Who has the Supreme Court barred from suppressing free speech, according to the author?
2. What important issues are highlighted by sexual speech that "degrades" or "subordinates" women, according to Strossen?
3. In the author's opinion, how would restricting speech that conveys sexist ideas threaten other forms of speech?

Martin Luther King, Malcolm X
Freedom of speech is as good as sex.

—Madonna, performer

Since Christianity . . . concentrated on sexual behavior as the
root of virtue, everything pertaining to sex has been a "special
case" in our culture, evoking peculiarly inconsistent attitudes.

—Susan Sontag, writer

While Madonna believes that free speech and sex are equally
good, many other Americans believe that they are equally
bad—at least when the speech is *about* sex. Therefore, just as the
American legal system has outlawed certain types of sexual activity—even by consenting adults in private—it has outlawed certain types of sexual expression—again, even by or for consent-
ing adults in private. This sexual prudery in American law reflects our Puritan heritage. Garrison Keillor made this point with characteristic hu-
mor in his 1990 congressional testimony supporting the National Endowment for the Arts, which was embattled because it
had funded certain sexually oriented works, including Robert
Mapplethorpe's homoerotic photographs. Keillor said: "My an-
cestors were Puritans from England, [who] arrived here in 1648
in the hope of finding greater restrictions than were permissible
under English law at the time."

THE SEXUAL EXPRESSION EXCEPTION

The First Amendment's broadly phrased free speech guarantee—"Congress shall make no law . . . abridging the freedom of
speech"—contains no exception for sexual expression. (Although the First Amendment expressly prohibits only congressional laws that abridge free speech, the Supreme Court has interpreted it as implicitly prohibiting any government action that
abridges free speech. Moreover, the Court has held that the First
Amendment bars private citizens from invoking the legal system—for example, through private lawsuits—to suppress free
speech.) Nevertheless, the Supreme Court has consistently read
such an exception into the First Amendment, allowing sexual
speech to be restricted or even banned under circumstances in
which it would not allow other types of speech to be limited.
While American law is, overall, the most speech-protective in
the world, it is far less protective of sexual speech than the law
in some other countries. Our First Amendment jurisprudence,
along with everything else in our culture, as Susan Sontag suggests, treats sex as a "special case."

The very change in current law that procensorship feminists advocate—that it target sexual expression that "subordinates" or "degrades" women—highlights the important ideas that such speech conveys about significant public issues, notably, gender roles and gender-based discrimination. Consequently, the courts have recognized that the subset of sexual speech that the Andrea Dworkin–Catharine MacKinnon faction seeks to suppress, as distinct from the subset of sexual speech that is unprotected under current obscenity doctrine, is really "political" speech, which has traditionally received the highest level of legal protection.

The MacDworkinite concept of pornography, in focusing expressly on the political ideas conveyed by sexual expression, would necessarily threaten other forms of political expression, too. In contrast, the Court's concept of obscene expression focuses specifically on the alleged lack of ideas conveyed by such speech. At least in theory, then, obscenity is a self-contained category of sexual expression whose unprotected status does not directly threaten other speech. As I will explain, in practice the concept of obscenity cannot be cabined, and does threaten valuable expression. But the alternative, more expansive notion of pornography-as-discrimination even more directly threatens a broader range of speech, as well as many core free speech principles.

THE SPREAD OF CENSORSHIP

If we should restrict sexually explicit speech because it purveys sexist ideas, as the feminist antipornography faction argues, then why shouldn't we restrict non–sexually explicit speech when it purveys sexist ideas? And if speech conveying sexist ideas can be restricted, then why shouldn't speech be restricted when it conveys racist, heterosexist, and other biased ideas? These logically indistinguishable applications of the feminist antipornography analysis lead many in the Dworkin-MacKinnon camp, including Dworkin and MacKinnon themselves, to advocate restricting racist and other forms of "hate" speech.

Yet the Supreme Court has repeatedly held that the First Amendment protects not only speech that is full of hate on the speaker's part, but also speech that is hateful to its audience. As former justice Oliver Wendell Holmes declared, "[I]f there is any principle of the Constitution that more imperatively calls for attachment than any other it is the principle of free thought—not free thought for those who agree with us but freedom for the thought we hate.'"

Furthermore, the Supreme Court has consistently rejected calls for censoring (nonobscene) speech when there is no demonstrable, direct causal link between the speech and immediate harm. But this is the feminist procensorship argument in a nutshell—that pornography should be suppressed based on speculation that it may lead to discrimination or violence against women in the long run, despite the lack of evidence to substantiate these fears. If we should restrict pornography on this basis, then why shouldn't we suppress any expression that might ultimately have a negative effect?

FREE SPEECH IN JEOPARDY

If MacDworkinism should prevail in the courts, it would jeopardize all of the foregoing free speech precedents and principles. The government could outlaw flag burning and the teaching of Marxist doctrine because they might lead to the erosion of patriotism and our capitalist system; white supremacist and black nationalist speeches could be criminalized because they might lead to racial segregation; peaceful demonstrations for (or against) civil rights, women's rights, gay rights, and, indeed, any other potentially controversial causes could be banned because they might provoke violent counterdemonstrations; advertising for alcohol, tobacco, and innumerable other products could be prohibited because it might cause adverse health effects; feminist expression could be stifled because it might threaten "traditional family values" and the attendant domestic order and tranquillity; abortion clinic advertising and other prochoice expression could be suppressed because it might lead to the termination of potential life; indeed, feminist antipornography advocacy could itself be suppressed because it could endanger cherished constitutional rights! The list is literally endless.

Make no mistake: if accepted, the feminist procensorship analysis would lead inevitably to the suppression of far more than pornography. At stake is all sexually oriented speech, any expression that allegedly subordinates or undermines the equality of any group, and any speech that may have a tendency to lead to any kind of harm. One might well ask about the feminist procensorship philosophy, not what expression would be stifled, but rather, what expression would be safe.

Periodical Bibliography

The following articles have been selected to supplement the diverse views presented in this chapter. Addresses are provided for periodicals not indexed in the *Readers' Guide to Periodical Literature*, the *Alternative Press Index*, the *Social Sciences Index*, or the *Index to Legal Periodicals and Books*.

William F. Buckley	"Burn the Flag? Well, No," *National Review*, July 10, 1995.
Steven Hill	"Speech May Be Free, but It Sure Isn't Cheap," *Humanist*, May/June 1994.
Molly Ivins	"Even Racists Have Right to Free Speech," *Liberal Opinion Week*, September 29, 1997. Available from PO Box 468, Vinton, IA 52349.
Wendy Kaminer	"God's Stars and Stripes: A Burning Issue?" *Nation*, April 28, 1997.
Roger Kimball	"Uncensored and Unashamed," *Index on Censorship*, May/June 1996.
Virginia Lam	"Illiberal Arts: Campus Censorship," *World & I*, January 1998. Available from 25 Beacon St., Boston, MA 02108-2803.
Anthony Lewis	"Nanny Knows Best," *Index on Censorship*, September/October 1995.
Nation	Special section: "Speech and Power: Is First Amendment Absolutism Obsolete?" July 21, 1997.
Charley Reese	"Free Speech Doesn't Protect Lying," *Conservative Chronicle*, February 11, 1998. Available from Box 37077, Boone, IA 50037-0077.
Chi Chi Sileo	"Pornographobia: Feminists Go to War," *Insight*, February 27, 1995. Available from 3600 New York Ave. NE, Washington, DC 20002.
Cass R. Sunstein	"Is Violent Speech a Right?" *American Prospect*, Summer 1995.
Joan Kennedy Taylor	"Child Pornography and Free Speech," *Liberty*, January 1997. Available from PO Box 1181, Port Townsend, WA 98368.
Mark Tushnet	"New Meaning for First Amendment," *ABA Journal*, November 1995.
Thomas G. West	"Freedom of Speech: Is America at High Tide . . . or Low?" *American Enterprise*, March/April 1996.

IS THE RIGHT TO PRIVACY THREATENED?

CHAPTER PREFACE

In June 1990, Ruth Shulman and her family were returning from Palm Springs, California, to their home in Santa Monica when the car she was riding in crashed and overturned in a ditch along the freeway. Shulman was seriously injured and pinned inside the car. The paramedics who worked to free her were wearing microphones. The helicopter that brought her to the hospital emergency room had on board a crew from a real-life rescue television show. When Shulman saw herself on TV three months later, begging the paramedics to let her die, she was stunned and outraged. She sued for invasion of privacy, charging that her tragedy was taped without her knowledge or consent.

Shulman is just one of dozens of people across the nation who claim that their privacy has been invaded by broadcasters who televised them without their permission. Shulman asks, "Who gives anyone the right to take my private life and put it on national TV if it isn't a news story?" She believes she had a valid expectation of a right to privacy at the accident scene since it had been closed off to everyone except emergency personnel. Seeing herself on television, and the possibility that her children and her mother might one day hear her urging paramedics to let her die, was "gruesome and upsetting," she asserts. Shulman's supporters contend that she and others like her should be allowed to keep their most tragic moments private.

Media lawyers fear that if the court rules in Shulman's favor, the freedom of the press would be restricted. They argue that since the broadcast was truthful, it should be protected by the First Amendment, regardless of the event's newsworthiness or offensiveness. Freedom of the press is "a basic constitutional guarantee, and it has to be protected zealously, and it has to be protected even when it is unpopular," asserts a lawyer for the television show. The California Supreme Court was expected to rule on Shulman's case in 1998.

Both sides agree that the right to privacy is a fundamental right, but they disagree on which circumstances should be protected by this right. In the following chapter, the authors question whether the loss of the right to privacy is harmful or beneficial and whether the right to privacy is threatened in today's society.

"Giving up some measure of privacy is exactly what the common good requires."

A LOSS OF PRIVACY BENEFITS SOCIETY

Amitai Etzioni

Amitai Etzioni is a professor at George Washington University in Washington, D.C., and is the editor of the *Responsive Community*, a quarterly communitarian journal. In the following viewpoint, Etzioni argues that with the development of new technology, it will be increasingly more difficult to protect people's right to privacy. However, Etzioni contends, a loss of privacy actually benefits society by exposing criminals to public scrutiny.

As you read, consider the following questions:

1. According to Etzioni, what is the only way that old-fashioned privacy can be restored?
2. How does the author counter charges that fingerprinting welfare recipients will stigmatize them?
3. What guidelines does Etzioni suggest for additional limits on the right to privacy?

Reprinted from Amitai Etzioni, "Less Privacy Is Good for Us (and You)," *Responsive Community*, Summer 1996, by permission of the publisher.

At first you are horrified. Your remaining shreds of privacy are being peeled off of you as if you are caught in a nightmarish forced striptease. Neighbors listen in on your cellular phone. Your boss taps into your e-mail and medical records. A reporter easily pulls up on his home computer which video tapes you rented, what you paid for with your credit card, and with whom you traveled to Acapulco. Furiously you seek new laws to protect yourself from data rape.

THE GENIE IS OUT OF THE BOTTLE

Not so fast. Our ability to restore old-fashioned privacy is about the same as our ability to vanquish nuclear weapons. Once the genie of high-power computers and communication technologies has been let out of the bottle, no one can cork it again. We must either return to the Stone Age—pay cash, use carrier pigeons, forget insurance—or learn to live with shrunken privacy. Laws already on the books mainly foster a Prohibition-like effect: those keen to read your dossier do so *sub rosa* rather than in broad daylight.

Most important, *giving up some measure of privacy is exactly what the common good requires.* And, with some good will, we can mitigate the intrusive consequences. Take first a non-inflammatory case. Would you like Americans to be required to put out garbage in see-through bags, as residents of Tokyo are? You would if you realized that transparent bags help ensure that people will separate glass and cans from the rest of their trash. (If a person is keen to hide, say, used condoms from neighbors, he can put them in a paper bag within the clear bag.)

But what about more provocative cases, such as fingerprinting those who receive welfare checks? Such a practice makes them feel like criminals, civil libertarians complain. But would you rather continue a system in which numerous individuals *each* collect several welfare, unemployment, and Social Security checks? Moreover, once fingerprinting is widely applied, the stigma will wane. Students are already routinely fingerprinted when they take the LSATs.

Keeping computerized data about physicians who have been kicked out of hospitals maintains a record that shadows them long after they have paid their dues. But would you rather return to the world we had until recently, in which doctors who killed several patients due to gross negligence in New Jersey could cross the state lines and repeat their performance with impunity? (The databank records only that a physician has been forced to leave "for a cause.")

Child care centers and schools can now find out if security personnel they hire have a record of child abuse, a civil libertarian's nightmare. But would you rather have your child in a facility like the one in Orlando, Florida, where a guard made sexual advances to boys, because management learned only after the fact that he was previously convicted of raping a 14-year-old? (Such people are entitled to jobs, but, in my book, not attending to children.) And while most of us would rather not have our sexual preferences advertised, we support the new Megan's law that allows parents to find out when their new neighbor is a convicted child molester.

| USING SURVEILLANCE TO KEEP THE BABY SAFE

Every morning, when the couple left their Long Island home for work, they handed their 10-month-old daughter over to a nanny. They had liked the woman at first, but lately she seemed a little sloppy and neglectful. Still, they weren't entirely sure.

The couple opted for a novel solution: They hired a local business to wire the main playroom for audio and video. The tapes, recorded by a camera smaller than a beeper hidden behind a clock, confirmed their suspicions. While the baby cried and crawled around, the nanny watched soaps. The next day, they fired her.

Nicole Gaouette, *Christian Science Monitor*, June 24, 1996.

Does it make sense, in the hallowed name of privacy, to allow both deadbeat fathers and students who default on their loans to draw a salary from a government agency, just to avoid the use of computer cross-checks? Would you rather allow banks to hide the movements of large amounts of cash, or curb drug lords' transactions? Would you rather be treated with an antibiotic to which you are allergic as you are wheeled into an emergency room, or have a new health card (in your possession) display a warning?

THE WAY TO AVOID A POLICE STATE

Will all these new knowledge technologies lead to a police state, as civil libertarians constantly warn us? As I see it, the shortest way to tyranny runs the other way around: If we do not significantly improve our ability to reduce violent crime, sexual abuse, and to stem epidemics, an ever-larger number of Americans will demand strong-armed authorities to restore law and order. Already too many desperate fellow citizens are all too ready to "suspend the Constitution until the war against drugs is won." Let us allow the new capabilities of cyberspace help restore civil order, which is at the foundation of ordered liberties.

We are properly distressed when we are denied credit, or learn that the wrong person has been arrested, because of mistakes in databanks. But this is not the effect of a violation of privacy. It is the consequence of data poorly collected and sloppily maintained. We urgently need quicker and easier ways to make corrections in our dossiers, rather than to try to ban largely beneficial new information technologies just because they need fine tuning. Congress should pass the Ombudsperson Office Law to this effect. Better yet, rather than wait until complaints are filed, it should proactively test samples of files to ensure that error rates are low and corrections expeditious.

Once one accepts that privacy is not an absolute value, we must look for the criteria that will guide us when additional trimming of this basic good is suggested. Guidelines include the following: tolerate new limitations on privacy only when there is a compelling need (e.g., to reduce the spread of contagious disease); minimize the entailed intrusion (e.g., measure the temperature of a urine sample for drug tests, rather than observe as it is being produced); double check that there is no other way of serving the same purpose; and, minimize the side effects (e.g., insist that we be allowed to refuse junk mail).

Frankly, most of us would rather prevent others from peeping into our records, but we can readily see the merits of tracking data about other people. Well, they feel the same way about us. Let those who have never speeded, have always paid their taxes in full, or have no other reason to be under some form of social scrutiny, cast the first stone.

| "The right to privacy is essential to
the preservation of freedom."

A LOSS OF PRIVACY HARMS SOCIETY

Joseph S. Fulda

In the following viewpoint, Joseph S. Fulda argues that a society cannot be free if citizens do not have a right to privacy. Privacy is essential because a government that is ignorant of an individual's thoughts and deeds cannot act to impinge on his or her rights, he asserts. However, Fulda contends, the people's right to privacy has come under attack. Society should do everything it can to protect its right to privacy, he maintains. Fulda is a contributing editor of the *Freeman*, a monthly libertarian magazine.

As you read, consider the following questions:

1. What is the positive feedback loop for privacy, according to Fulda?
2. In the author's opinion, what is the most blatant governmental violation of a person's right to privacy?
3. How does money both protect and abridge privacy, according to the author?

Reprinted from Joseph S. Fulda, "Liberty and Privacy: Connections," *The Freeman*, December 1996, by permission of *The Freeman*.

If property is liberty's other half, privacy is its guardian. The right to privacy is essential to the preservation of freedom for the simplest of reasons. If no one knows what I do, when I do it, and with whom I do it, no one can possibly interfere with it. Intuitively, we understand this, as witness our drawing the curtains and pulling the window shades down when prowlers are about. The threat to freedom comes from both the criminal and the state, from any and all ways and means in which others forcibly overcome our will. Just as we do not want burglars casing our homes, we should fear the government's intimate knowledge of the many details of our daily lives.

Although equally critical to liberty, privacy rights, unlike property rights, are not enumerated in the Constitution (except for the fourth amendment's protection of "persons, houses, papers, and effects" from unreasonable searches), although throughout most of our history Americans have retained their right to privacy. Today, however, this right is insecure as the courts, except in a few cases, have been unwilling to find in privacy a right retained by the people as suggested by the ninth amendment's declaration and . . . have been unwilling to bar legislated invasions of privacy on the grounds that they are simply outside the scope of the few and well-defined powers granted by the Constitution to the Congress.

Nor is privacy from the snoop afforded that much more protection today. Few, indeed, are the invasions of privacy regarded as criminal, rather than tortious, and many are not actionable at all. Paradoxically, the argument has been that one has a liberty to invade the privacy of others, if there is no reasonable expectation for that privacy. That may sound reasonable, but it forms what engineers term a positive feedback loop: The more privacy is invaded, the less reason one has to expect privacy, and therefore the more it may be invaded. This faulty jurisprudential theory has single-handedly eviscerated tort law and rendered the only specific privacy protection in the Bill of Rights—that barring unreasonable searches—weaker and weaker. The proper response to this flawed reasoning is simple: People often expect, in the sense of justly demand, what they cannot expect, in the sense of predict. We may thus have a right to expect our privacy to be respected in the former sense, whether or not we may expect it to be respected in the latter sense. Expectations, in other words, must be defined against a fixed standard of reasonableness, not one programmed to continuously decay.

The most egregious governmental violation of our privacy lies with our tax system, which is frankly frightening, as the potential for the destruction of liberty arising from the reams of information returned annually to the government is vast. The government is told our family size, our occupation, our business associates—employers, employees, contractors, partners, and the like (and, if we report barter income, some of our friends, as well), our holdings (unless we realize neither profit nor loss from their transfer and, also, gain no income while we continue our ownership), our schooling (unless it is not relevant to our work), and our provisions for retirement. Although no one may expect such dire consequences, the potential exists for such diverse state initiatives as population control programs, mandatory occupational tracks, massive interference with freedom of association, and enforcement of any or all of these by threat of loss of our holdings. Without this tax-related information, such interferences would be impossible. It is no accident that totalitarian systems in which there is no freedom whatsoever also tolerate no privacy. For Big Brother to act, he must know, and state surveillance with spies everywhere was a staple of the now-fallen totalitarian regimes.

PRIVACY PROTECTS FREEDOM

A primary moral foundation for the value of privacy is its role as a condition of freedom: A shield of privacy is absolutely essential if one is freely to pursue his or her projects or cultivate intimate social relationships.

If people know that I am watching them, compiling a record of their activities or monitoring their conversations, they are apt to be more self-conscious and preoccupied with whether their statements or actions meet my approval. Besides causing such inhibitions, those who violate our private space by acquiring confidential information without permission may use it to exercise control over our activities.

Richard A. Spinello, *America*, January 4, 1997.

Nor are these concerns the idle musings of a libertarian alarmist. Buried deep in the pages of the Federal Register is news that the Internal Revenue Service (IRS) is implementing a massive new initiative, styled Compliance 2000. At the heart of the initiative is "a huge database" with "personal information on every American" gathered from records kept by "other federal agencies, state and local authorities, private organizations and the media." The regulation giving notice of this massive new database, composed of records from cyberspace as well as more traditional sources, stated that Compliance 2000 is "exempt from the notification, access, and content provisions of the Privacy Act [1974]." In other words, "[t]his means that the IRS doesn't need permission to get information, doesn't need to show it to you, and doesn't need to correct the information even if it's wrong." Privacy groups such as EPIC (Electronic Privacy Information Center) and business groups such as the DMA (Direct Marketing Association) strenuously opposed the initiative, but it went forward anyway. The IRS hopes to look at what is consumed as a check on the self-reporting of what is produced, but the potential for abuse and, according to the DMA, for chilling legitimate businesses is obviously vast.

And, just as the state, in this initiative and more generally, threatens privacy, the market protects it. Consider the market institution of money. Money must be portable, durable, and limited in quantity but the value of money lies not only in what it can buy, but also in its protection of privacy. Under a barter regime, everyone I buy from knows what I produce, and everyone I sell to knows what I consume. In the cash economy, only my customers know what I produce and only those from whom I purchase know what I consume. That is why the black-market cash economies of the once-totalitarian regimes of Eastern Europe were synonymous with the bits and pieces of freedom that survived there. Of course, cash transactions protect privacy from the snoop as well as from the state. With my bank-issued Master-Card number, for example, any mail-order merchant can find out the sum of my purchases and cash advances, my last payment, my next due date and minimum amount due, and my credit line, for all it takes is the credit card number and my zip code, the former of which he must have to claim payment and the latter of which he must have to deliver the goods.

To a lesser extent, even the serial numbers on paper money abridge privacy, as those who engage in businesses the feds do not approve of, such as the drug trade, have found out. Bank holdings are even more vulnerable, because upon transfer of large amounts of cash from accounts (marked with an ever-present Taxpayer Identification Number), the government is immediately notified. The new industry now known as money-laundering provides nothing but privacy-protection services to the rather large market spawned by various federal prohibitions—and this simple fact holds, whatever one's opinion of the nature of the enterprises whose privacy is being protected.

Privacy is the great shield of freedom from interference. Everyone who savors freedom will champion the right to privacy.

> "Now that privacy cannot easily be created by simple physical space, it is all the more important to insure the existence of private enclaves . . . through new law."

MORE LAWS ARE NEEDED TO PROTECT PRIVACY

Cass R. Sunstein

Diana, the Princess of Wales, was killed in August 1997 in a car crash as she was being pursued by photographers who were trying to take her picture. In the following viewpoint, Cass R. Sunstein argues that while some laws protect celebrities from unwanted attention, more laws are needed to keep their privacy from being invaded. Additional laws protecting the privacy of celebrities would benefit everyone else as well, he maintains. Sunstein is a professor at the University of Chicago Law School and the author of Democracy and the Problem of Free Speech.

As you read, consider the following questions:

1. According to Sunstein, what existing laws can help protect a person's right to privacy?
2. In what ways can the states do more to protect the right to privacy, in the author's opinion?
3. What two reasons does Sunstein give for why society should protect a celebrity's right to privacy?

The death of Diana, Princess of Wales, has left us with difficult questions about the relationship between free speech and privacy: Does the law allow celebrities to protect themselves from harassment? And should the law do more? The answer to both is an emphatic yes. Existing laws can help insure privacy, but the time has come for some creative thinking about other possibilities.

EXISTING LAWS

Everyone, even the most famous people, can use laws against trespass to prevent intrusions on private property and the law of libel to protect against intentional or reckless falsehoods. Most states provide other protections as well. It is generally grounds for a lawsuit, for example, if someone intrudes on your private domain by eavesdropping electronically or wiretapping.

The law also prohibits using a celebrity's name in advertising without permission. A cereal company cannot claim or suggest that Michael Jordan enjoys its product unless Mr. Jordan agrees.

In addition, state laws generally prohibit news organizations from placing people in a "false light in the public eye." A newspaper can be sued if, for example, it prints a photograph of two famous people at dinner and wrongly implies that they are romantically involved. Many states also restrict public disclosure of private facts, even if what is said is true.

The free-speech arguments being heard in the aftermath of Diana's death have, of course, already been used against these existing laws. And in general, courts have concluded that such privacy protections do not violate the First Amendment.

The First Amendment is not an absolute, courts have said, and it allows states some room to restrict speech in the interest of safeguarding privacy. Even if trespass law interferes with what the press would like to do, it is hardly unconstitutional, and commercial exploitation of celebrities' names can be banned without offending the First Amendment.

Harder constitutional questions arise when states allow claims involving "false light" and the disclosure of private facts. The Supreme Court has said surprisingly little about those questions. In its only major ruling on the subject, 30 years ago, the Court said that in "matters of public interest" the press had special latitude, but the Justices did not define their terms. Among the things that remain uncertain is the extent to which state law can protect the privacy of television stars and athletes, as opposed to elected officials.

It is in such areas that the law could do more. Some states

might build on their existing laws to create a firmer wall of privacy around people who do not want to be exploited, harassed or humiliated. States might, for example, try specifically forbidding photographers to invade a private domain through the use of long-distance photographic equipment. They might allow people to recover damages if they have been repeatedly harassed about a personal tragedy. They might make it a misdemeanor to publish photographs taken without permission in a home or other private domain.

THE BEST BET

The threats to privacy in American society have become so pervasive that federal and state laws simply have not kept up. And it does little good to pass new narrowly targeted privacy laws— covering, say, medical records or, perhaps, employment records— because new privacy issues emerge every day.

The best bet is a federal privacy law that applies to both the government and private sector. It should set parameters on the kind of information that may be legally obtained on an individual, how it may be used and by whom.

Joseph Perkins, *San Diego Union-Tribune*, September 12, 1997.

In such experiments, however, a good deal of creativity and care is required. Broadly drawn laws would create problems. For example, the First Amendment would almost certainly bar any law that might have been used to forbid the publication of the famous photographs of Gary Hart with Donna Rice. These kinds of hurdles, though, should not discourage experimentation, because it is perfectly legitimate for states to experiment with new ways to adapt to social and technological change.

TWO REASONS TO CARE

All this leaves a final question: Why should the rest of us care about intrusions on the privacy of celebrities and other famous people, hardly the most disadvantaged members of society? There are two reasons.

First, a democracy is badly served when newspapers and television focus so intensely on the personal joys and tragedies of famous people. This kind of "news" crowds out more serious issues, and there is an important difference—as the Constitution's framers well knew, and as many people today appear to have forgotten—between the public interest and what interests the public.

Second, intrusions on the privacy of celebrities are, at least potentially, intrusions on the privacy of everyone. New technology is making it extremely difficult for both celebrities and ordinary people to insulate themselves from public view, especially at their most vulnerable moments.

People who have lost a house or a child or a spouse are often unable to grieve privately, simply because of the persistence of someone who wants to exploit their tragedy. Now that privacy cannot easily be created by simple physical space, it is all the more important to insure the existence of private enclaves, through changes in attitude or, if necessary, through new law. If famous people are unable to protect themselves against public inspection of their private lives, the same may eventually be true for the rest of us.

"Every state already provides civil remedies for those who believe their privacy has been violated."

MORE LAWS ARE NOT NEEDED TO PROTECT PRIVACY

Jane E. Kirtley

The term "paparazzi," which often has negative connotations, refers to photographers who pursue celebrities in order to take candid photographs of them. In the following viewpoint, Jane E. Kirtley argues that passing laws to restrict the actions of paparazzi who harass celebrities, such as those who were chasing Princess Diana when she was killed in a car crash in August 1997, would violate the First Amendment. Distinguishing between "legitimate" news gatherers and paparazzi would be impossible, she contends, and would lead to a suppression of dissent. Those whose rights to privacy are truly violated have options to seek redress under civil laws, she maintains. Kirtley, a lawyer and former newspaper reporter, is the executive director of the Reporters Committee for Freedom of the Press in Arlington, Virginia.

As you read, consider the following questions:
1. What are some laws suggested to protect celebrities' right to privacy, as cited by the author?
2. In Kirtley's opinion, what laws already protect the privacy of celebrities?
3. What is legislation aimed at curbing the paparazzi really concerned about, according to the author?

Reprinted from Jane E. Kirtley, "Risky Control Notions," The Washington Times, September 14, 1997, by permission of Scripps Howard News Service.

After the shocking death of Princess Diana, the blame game began. Who better to condemn than the paparazzi, those rogue photojournalists who dog the rich and famous in hopes of snapping the elusive million-dollar shot? Forget the fact that the public gobbles up salacious pictures by the dozen, or that news organizations of every stripe cater to that insatiable appetite. In the wake of the death of a princess, the establishment news media rushed to distinguish themselves from the "gutter press" and the guttersnipes who feed it, and celebrities and politicians colluded to launch an assault on the First Amendment.

SUGGESTED LEGISLATION

Various self-serving individuals insist that celebrities represent some kind of endangered species, whose pampered lives are made a living hell by the surveillance of free-lance photographers. Legislation is needed to create "buffer zones" to insulate the poor things from unwanted press attention and to ratchet up the penalties for intrusions into "personal space."

One security expert contends that paparazzi should be required to obtain permits before plying their trade, and a former publicist for the late Dodi Fayed said a "Son of Sam" law should make it a crime to photograph an unwilling subject, and allow the state to confiscate any profits as the financial fruits of such "crimes."

Virtually everyone who proposes these laws insists they will apply only to the paparazzi—not to legitimate news gatherers. But no one has explained who will decide which media are "legitimate."

The lines between tabloid and establishment press are none too clear. The explosion of new technology means anyone with a cheap videocam and a modem can become an international publisher. And government licenses can easily be used to silence opposition journalism. Any law that discriminates between categories of news gatherers is doomed to succumb to a First Amendment challenge.

Criminal conduct, on the other hand, has never been protected by the First Amendment. Many of the tactics used by the paparazzi could be punished under existing statutes outlawing trespass, stalking, or recklessly endangering others. Every state already provides civil remedies for those who believe their privacy has been violated.

Since 1890, when Louis Brandeis defined privacy as "the right to be left alone," courts have struggled to reconcile that individual "right" with the constitutionally guaranteed rights of the news media to vigorously report on politicians, sports figures and movie stars—most of whom would certainly prefer that their personal and financial peccadilloes be left uncovered.

Marshall Ramsey. Reprinted by permission of Copley News Service.

In the United States, privacy law evolved primarily through the common law. Court cases are flexible enough to accommodate these competing interests because they allow a judge to balance individual rights against the newsworthiness of a particular subject, resulting in an equitable outcome most of the time.

But in France, home of the most restrictive privacy statutes in the world, the rich and powerful use court orders to stop publication of just about anything they don't like, and to collect hefty damages in the bargain. This lethal combination has cowed the French media to the point that investigative journalism is almost unknown there. But it still didn't prevent the crash in the Paris tunnel.

TASTE AND CONTROL

A growing movement has advocated similar laws in this country. In the name of protecting privacy, a proposed California law would make it illegal to photograph an accident scene. Such a statute might seem edifying, because it would shield the public from some grisly pictures. But it would also mean they could only learn the "official story."

Considered in that light, the news value of the photographs

that the paparazzi took of Princess Diana's accident scene becomes clear because those "prurient" pictures might hold the answers to some of the nagging questions that still surround the events of that tragic night.

Legislation aimed at curbing the paparazzi can't withstand constitutional scrutiny because it is really about taste and control, not privacy. The First Amendment decrees that the government can't dictate what the public has a right to know. Neither should publicists to the stars.

"Students who voluntarily participate
in school athletics have reason to
expect intrusions upon normal rights
and privileges, including privacy."

RANDOM DRUG TESTS ON STUDENT-ATHLETES DO NOT VIOLATE THE RIGHT TO PRIVACY

Antonin Scalia et al.

Antonin Scalia is a justice on the U.S. Supreme Court. In the following viewpoint, Scalia, joined by chief justice William Rehnquist and justices Anthony Kennedy, Clarence Thomas, Ruth Bader Ginsburg, and Stephen Breyer, finds that random drug searches of student athletes do not violate their right to privacy. Student athletes are subjected to more regulations than other students and should not expect the same level of privacy, the justices contend. Furthermore, the authors agree that the school has a compelling interest in testing the student athletes for drugs, and therefore violation of their privacy is justified.

As you read, consider the following questions:

1. What is the Fourth Amendment's ultimate measure of the constitutionality of a government search, according to the authors?
2. When can a search still be considered reasonable even if it is not supported by a warrant or probable cause, in the authors' opinion?
3. According to the justices, in what ways are the privacy expectations of student athletes infringed upon in the school setting?

Reprinted from the majority opinion of the Supreme Court of the United States (including Justices Antonin Scalia, William Rehnquist, Anthony Kennedy, Clarence Thomas, Ruth Bader Ginsburg, and Stephen Breyer) in the decision of *Vernonia School District 47J v. Acton*, June 26, 1995.

Petitioner Vernonia School District 47J (District) operates one high school and three grade schools in the logging community of Vernonia, Oregon. As elsewhere in small-town America, school sports play a prominent role in the town's life, and student athletes are admired in their schools and in the community.

DRUG PROBLEMS IN THE SCHOOLS

Drugs had not been a major problem in Vernonia schools. In the mid-to-late 1980's, however, teachers and administrators observed a sharp increase in drug use. Students began to speak out about their attraction to the drug culture, and to boast that there was nothing the school could do about it. Along with more drugs came more disciplinary problems. Between 1988 and 1989 the number of disciplinary referrals in Vernonia schools rose to more than twice the number reported in the early 1980's, and several students were suspended. Students became increasingly rude during class; outbursts of profane language became common.

Not only were student athletes included among the drug users but, as the District Court found, athletes were the leaders of the drug culture. This caused the District's administrators particular concern, since drug use increases the risk of sports-related injury. Expert testimony at the trial confirmed the deleterious effects of drugs on motivation, memory, judgment, reaction, coordination, and performance. The high school football and wrestling coach witnessed a severe sternum injury suffered by a wrestler, and various omissions of safety procedures and misexecutions by football players, all attributable in his belief to the effects of drug use.

Initially, the District responded to the drug problem by offering special classes, speakers, and presentations designed to deter drug use. It even brought in a specially trained dog to detect drugs, but the drug problem persisted. According to the District Court:

> [T]he administration was at its wits end and . . . a large segment of the student body, particularly those involved in interscholastic athletics, was in a state of rebellion. Disciplinary problems had reached "epidemic proportions." The coincidence of an almost three-fold increase in classroom disruptions and disciplinary reports along with the staff's direct observations of students using drugs or glamorizing drug and alcohol use led the administration to the inescapable conclusion that the rebellion was being fueled by alcohol and drug abuse as well as the student's misperceptions about the drug culture.

90

At that point, District officials began considering a drug-testing program. They held a parent "input night" to discuss the proposed Student Athlete Drug Policy (Policy), and the parents in attendance gave their unanimous approval. The school board approved the Policy for implementation in the fall of 1989. Its expressed purpose is to prevent student athletes from using drugs, to protect their health and safety, and to provide drug users with assistance programs.

THE DRUG TESTS

The Policy applies to all students participating in interscholastic athletics. Students wishing to play sports must sign a form consenting to the testing and must obtain the written consent of their parents. Athletes are tested at the beginning of the season for their sport. In addition, once each week of the season the names of the athletes are placed in a "pool" from which a student, with the supervision of two adults, blindly draws the names of 10% of the athletes for random testing. Those selected are notified and tested that same day, if possible.

The student to be tested completes a specimen control form which bears an assigned number. Prescription medications that the student is taking must be identified by providing a copy of the prescription or a doctor's authorization. The student then enters an empty locker room accompanied by an adult monitor of the same sex. Each boy selected produces a sample at a urinal, remaining fully clothed with his back to the monitor, who stands approximately 12 to 15 feet behind the student. Monitors may (though do not always) watch the student while he produces the sample, and they listen for normal sounds of urination. Girls produce samples in an enclosed bathroom stall, so that they can be heard but not observed. After the sample is produced, it is given to the monitor, who checks it for temperature and tampering and then transfers it to a vial.

The samples are sent to an independent laboratory, which routinely tests them for amphetamines, cocaine, and marijuana. Other drugs, such as LSD, may be screened at the request of the District, but the identity of a particular student does not determine which drugs will be tested. The laboratory's procedures are 99.94% accurate. The District follows strict procedures regarding the chain of custody and access to test results. The laboratory does not know the identity of the students whose samples it tests. It is authorized to mail written test reports only to the superintendent and to provide test results to District personnel by telephone only after the requesting official recites a code confirming his authority. Only the superintendent, principals, vice-principals, and athletic directors have access to test results, and the results are not kept for more than one year. If a sample tests positive, a second test is administered as soon as possible to confirm the result. If the second test is negative, no further action is taken. If the second test is positive, the athlete's parents are notified, and the school principal convenes a meeting with the student and his parents, at which the student is given the option of (1) participating for six weeks in an assistance program that includes weekly urinalysis, or (2) suffering suspension from athletics for the remainder of the current season and the next athletic season. The student is then retested prior to the start of the next athletic season for which he or she is eligible. The Policy states that a second offense results in automatic imposition of option (2); a third offense in suspension for the remainder of the current season and the next two athletic seasons.

THE LAWSUIT

In the fall of 1991, respondent James Acton, then a seventh-grader, signed up to play football at one of the District's grade schools. He was denied participation, however, because he and his parents refused to sign the testing consent forms. The Actons filed suit, seeking declaratory and injunctive relief from enforcement of the Policy on the grounds that it violated the Fourth and Fourteenth Amendments to the United States Constitution and Article I, 9, of the Oregon Constitution. After a bench trial, the District Court entered an order denying the claims on the merits and dismissing the action. The United States Court of Appeals for the Ninth Circuit reversed, holding that the Policy violated both the Fourth and Fourteenth Amendments and Article I, 9, of the Oregon Constitution. We granted certiorari.

THE FOURTH AMENDMENT

The Fourth Amendment to the United States Constitution provides that the Federal Government shall not violate "[t]he right of the people to be secure in their persons, houses, papers, and effects, against unreasonable searches and seizures, . . ." We have held that the Fourteenth Amendment extends this constitutional guarantee to searches and seizures by state officers, [Elkins v. United States (1960)], including public school officials, [New Jersey v. T.L.O. (1985)]. In Skinner v. Railway Labor Executives' Assn. we held that state-compelled collection and testing of urine, such as that required by the Student Athlete Drug Policy, constitutes a "search" subject to the demands of the Fourth Amendment.

As the text of the Fourth Amendment indicates, the ultimate measure of the constitutionality of a governmental search is "reasonableness." At least in a case such as this, where there was no clear practice, either approving or disapproving the type of search at issue, at the time the constitutional provision was enacted, we found in *Skinner*, (quoting *Delaware v. Prouse* [1979]), that whether a particular search meets the reasonableness standard "'is judged by balancing its intrusion on the individual's Fourth Amendment interests against its promotion of legitimate governmental interests.'" Where a search is undertaken by law enforcement officials to discover evidence of criminal wrongdoing, this Court has said that reasonableness generally requires the obtaining of a judicial warrant. Warrants cannot be issued, of course, without the showing of probable cause required by the Warrant Clause. But a warrant is not required to establish the reasonableness of all government searches; and when a warrant is not required (and the Warrant Clause therefore not applicable), probable cause is not invariably required either. A search unsupported by probable cause can be constitutional, we . . . said in *Griffin v. Wisconsin* (1987), "when special needs, beyond the normal need for law enforcement, make the warrant and probable-cause requirement impracticable."

| NOT AN ABSOLUTE RIGHT

Students at public institutions have not abandoned their constitutional rights at the schoolhouse door. The Constitution protects them from "unreasonable" searches. . . .

[However], Fourth Amendment rights are not absolute. They must be balanced against an overriding public interest. . . .

A right to privacy, to be sure, is a valuable right, but . . . the university's random testing program is a small invasion when balanced against a large problem. In any event, those who live locker room lives have mighty little privacy left to protect.

James K. Kilpatrick, *Conservative Chronicle*, June 22, 1994.

We have found such "special needs" to exist in the public-school context. There, as the District Court noted, the warrant requirement "would unduly interfere with the maintenance of the swift and informal disciplinary procedures [that are] needed," and "strict adherence to the requirement that searches be based upon probable cause" would undercut, as we ruled in T.L.O., "the substantial need of teachers and administrators for freedom to maintain order in the schools." The school search we approved in T.L.O., while not based on probable cause, was based on individualized suspicion of wrongdoing. As we explicitly acknowledged in T.L.O. (quoting *United States v. Martinez-Fuerte* [1976]), however, "'the Fourth Amendment imposes no irreducible requirement of such suspicion.'" We have upheld suspicionless searches and seizures to conduct drug testing of railroad personnel involved in train accidents; to conduct random drug testing of federal customs officers who carry arms or are involved in drug interdiction; and to maintain automobile checkpoints looking for illegal immigrants and contraband and drunk drivers. . . .

FOURTH AMENDMENT RIGHTS IN THE SCHOOLS

Fourth Amendment rights, no less than First and Fourteenth Amendment rights, are different in public schools than elsewhere; the "reasonableness" inquiry cannot disregard the schools' custodial and tutelary responsibility for children. For their own good and that of their classmates, public school children are routinely required to submit to various physical examinations, and to be vaccinated against various diseases. According to the American Academy of Pediatrics, most public schools "provide vision and hearing screening and dental and dermatological checks. . . . Others also mandate scoliosis screening at appropriate grade levels." In the 1991–1992 school year, all 50 States required public-school students to be vaccinated against diphtheria, measles, rubella, and polio. Therefore, we found in T.L.O. that, particularly with regard to medical examinations and procedures, . . . "students within the school environment have a lesser expectation of privacy than members of the population generally."

Legitimate privacy expectations are even less with regard to student athletes. School sports are not for the bashful. They require "suiting up" before each practice or event, and showering and changing afterwards. Public school locker rooms, the usual sites for these activities, are not notable for the privacy they afford. The locker rooms in Vernonia are typical: no individual dressing rooms are provided; shower heads are lined up along a wall, unseparated by any sort of partition or curtain; not even all the toilet stalls have doors. As the United States Court of Appeals for the Seventh Circuit has noted, there is "an element of 'communal undress' inherent in athletic participation."

There is an additional respect in which school athletes have a reduced expectation of privacy. By choosing to "go out for the team," they voluntarily subject themselves to a degree of regulation even higher than that imposed on students generally. In Vernonia's public schools, they must submit to a preseason physical exam (James testified that his included the giving of a urine sample), they must acquire adequate insurance coverage or sign an insurance waiver, maintain a minimum grade point average, and, according to the school district, comply with any "rules of conduct, dress, training hours and related matters as may be established for each sport by the head coach and athletic director with the principal's approval." Somewhat like adults who choose to participate in a "closely regulated industry," students who voluntarily participate in school athletics have reason to expect intrusions upon normal rights and privileges, including privacy.

THE DEGREE OF INTRUSION

Having considered the scope of the legitimate expectation of privacy at issue here, we turn next to the character of the intrusion that is complained of. We recognized in Skinner that collecting the samples for urinalysis intrudes upon "an excretory function traditionally shielded by great privacy." We noted, however, that the degree of intrusion depends upon the manner in which production of the urine sample is monitored. Under the District's Policy, male students produce samples at a urinal along a wall. They remain fully clothed and are only observed from behind, if at all. Female students produce samples in an enclosed stall, with a female monitor standing outside listening only for sounds of tampering. These conditions are nearly identical to those typically encountered in public restrooms, which men, women, and especially school children use daily. Under such conditions, the privacy interests compromised by the process of obtaining the urine sample are in our view negligible. The other privacy-invasive aspect of urinalysis is, of course, the information it discloses concerning the state of the subject's body, and the materials he has ingested. In this regard it is significant that the tests at issue here look only for drugs, and not for whether the student is, for example, epileptic, pregnant, or diabetic. Moreover, the drugs for which the samples are screened are standard, and do not vary according to the identity of the student. And finally, the results of the tests are disclosed only to a limited class of school personnel who have a need to know; and they are not turned over to law enforcement authorities or used for any internal disciplinary function. . . .

A COMPELLING INTEREST

Finally, we turn to consider the nature and immediacy of the governmental concern at issue here, and the efficacy of this means for meeting it. In both *Skinner* and *Treasury Employees v. Von Raab*, we characterized the government interest motivating the search as "compelling." Relying on these cases, the District Court held that because the District's program also called for drug testing in the absence of individualized suspicion, the District "must demonstrate a 'compelling need' for the program." The Court of Appeals appears to have agreed with this view. It is a mistake, however, to think that the phrase "compelling state interest," in the Fourth Amendment context, describes a fixed, minimum quantum of governmental concern, so that one can dispose of a case by answering in isolation the question: Is there a compelling state interest here? Rather, the phrase describes an interest which appears important enough to justify the particular search at hand, in light of other factors which show the search to be relatively intrusive upon a genuine expectation of privacy. Whether that relatively high degree of government concern is necessary in this case or not, we think it is met.

THE EFFECTS OF DRUGS ON STUDENTS

That the nature of the concern is important—indeed, perhaps compelling—can hardly be doubted. Deterring drug use by our Nation's schoolchildren is at least as important as enhancing efficient enforcement of the Nation's laws against the importation of drugs, which was the governmental concern in *Von Raab*, or deterring drug use by engineers and trainmen, which was the governmental concern in *Skinner*. School years are the time when the physical, psychological, and addictive effects of drugs are most severe. As Richard A. Hawley wrote, "Maturing nervous systems are more critically impaired by intoxicants than mature ones are; childhood losses in learning are lifelong and profound"; "children grow chemically dependent more quickly than adults, and their record of recovery is depressingly poor." And of course the effects of a drug-infested school are visited not just upon the users, but upon the entire student body and faculty, as the educational process is disrupted. In the present case, moreover, the necessity for the State to act is magnified by the fact that this evil is being visited not just upon individuals at large, but upon children for whom it has undertaken a special responsibility of care and direction. Finally, it must not be lost sight of that this program is directed more narrowly to drug use by school athletes, where the risk of immediate physical harm to the drug user or those with whom he is playing his sport is particularly high. Apart from psychological effects, which include impairment of judgment, slow reaction time, and a less-

96

ening of the perception of pain, the particular drugs screened by the District's Policy have been demonstrated to pose substantial physical risks to athletes. . . .

A CONSTITUTIONAL POLICY

Taking into account all the factors we have considered above—the decreased expectation of privacy, the relative unobtrusiveness of the search, and the severity of the need met by the search—we conclude Vernonia's Policy is reasonable and hence constitutional.

"The [school] District's suspicionless policy of testing all student-athletes sweeps too broadly ... to be reasonable under the Fourth Amendment."

RANDOM DRUG TESTS ON STUDENT-ATHLETES VIOLATE THE RIGHT TO PRIVACY

Sandra Day O'Connor, John Paul Stevens, and David Souter

Sandra Day O'Connor, John Paul Stevens, and David Souter are all justices of the U.S. Supreme Court. The following viewpoint is an excerpt of O'Connor's June 26, 1995, dissent from the majority opinion, which Stevens and Souter joined, concerning random drug tests of student athletes. O'Connor argues that testing randomly chosen student athletes for drugs without a suspicion of wrongdoing violates their right to privacy. The fact that the testing is broadly based does not lessen its unconstitutionality, she contends. The best way to protect a student's right to privacy, O'Connor asserts, is to perform drug tests only on those who can be reasonably suspected of using drugs.

As you read, consider the following questions:

1. Why is the Fourth Amendment interpreted more leniently in school searches, according to the author?
2. What message does suspicionless testing send to the tested students, as cited by O'Connor?
3. What reasons does the author give for objecting to using physical examinations and vaccinations as examples of searches?

Reprinted from the dissenting opinion of U.S. Supreme Court Justices Sandra Day O'Connor, John Paul Stevens, and David Souter in the decision of *Vernonia School District 47J v. Acton*, June 26, 1995.

The population of our Nation's public schools, grades 7 through 12, numbers around 18 million. By the reasoning of today's decision, the millions of these students who participate in interscholastic sports, an overwhelming majority of whom have given school officials no reason whatsoever to suspect they use drugs at school, are open to an intrusive bodily search.

THE DISSENT

In justifying this result, the Court dispenses with a requirement of individualized suspicion on considered policy grounds. First, it explains that precisely because every student athlete is being tested, there is no concern that school officials might act arbitrarily in choosing who to test. Second, a broad-based search regime, the Court reasons, dilutes the accusatory nature of the search. In making these policy arguments, of course, the Court sidesteps powerful, countervailing privacy concerns. In *Illinois v. Krull* (1987), Sandra Day O'Connor writes that blanket searches, because they can involve "thousands or millions" of searches, "pos[e] a greater threat to liberty" than do suspicion-based ones, which "affec[t] one person at a time." Searches based on individualized suspicion also afford potential targets considerable control over whether they will, in fact, be searched because a person can avoid such a search by not acting in an objectively suspicious way. And given that the surest way to avoid acting suspiciously is to avoid the underlying wrongdoing, the costs of such a regime, one would think, are minimal.

But whether a blanket search is "better" than a regime based on individualized suspicion is not a debate in which we should engage. In my view, it is not open to judges or government officials to decide on policy grounds which is better and which is worse. For most of our constitutional history, mass, suspicionless searches have been generally considered per se unreasonable within the meaning of the Fourth Amendment. And we have allowed exceptions in recent years only where it has been clear that a suspicion-based regime would be ineffectual. Because that is not the case here, I dissent. . . .

MASS SEARCHES AND CRIMINAL LAW

The view that mass, suspicionless searches, however evenhanded, are generally unreasonable remains inviolate in the criminal law enforcement context, at least where the search is more than minimally intrusive. It is worth noting in this regard that state-compelled, state-monitored collection and testing of urine, while perhaps not the most intrusive of searches, is still, according to Antonin Scalia, "particularly destructive of privacy and offensive to personal dignity." We have not hesitated to treat monitored bowel movements as highly intrusive (even in the special border search context); compare *United States v. Martinez-Fuerte* (1976) (brief interrogative stops of all motorists crossing certain border checkpoint reasonable without individualized suspicion), with *United States v. Montoya de Hernandez* (1985) (monitored bowel movement of border crossers reasonable only upon reasonable suspicion of alimentary canal smuggling), and it is not easy to draw a distinction. And certainly monitored urination combined with urine testing is more intrusive than some personal searches we have said trigger Fourth Amendment protections in the past. Finally, the collection and testing of urine is, of course, a search of a person, one of only four categories of suspect searches the Constitution mentions by name ("persons, houses, papers, and effects").

Thus, it remains the law that the police cannot, say, subject to drug testing every person entering or leaving a certain drug-ridden neighborhood in order to find evidence of crime. And this is true even though it is hard to think of a more compelling government interest than the need to fight the scourge of drugs on our streets and in our neighborhoods. Nor could it be otherwise, for if being evenhanded were enough to justify evaluating a search regime under an open-ended balancing test, the Warrant Clause, which presupposes that there is some category of searches for which individualized suspicion is non-negotiable, would be a dead letter. . . .

A SAFEGUARD AGAINST ABUSE

As an initial matter, I have serious doubts whether the Court is right that the District reasonably found that the lesser intrusion of a suspicion-based testing program outweighed its genuine concerns for the adversarial nature of such a program, and for its abuses. For one thing, there are significant safeguards against abuses. The fear that a suspicion-based regime will lead to the testing of "troublesome but not drug-likely" students, for example, ignores that the required level of suspicion in the school context is objectively reasonable suspicion. In this respect, the facts of our decision in *New Jersey v. T.L.O.* (1985) should be reassuring. There, we found reasonable suspicion to search a ninth-grade girl's purse for cigarettes after a teacher caught the girl smoking in the bathroom with a companion who admitted it. Moreover, any distress arising from what turns out to be a false accusation can be minimized by keeping the entire process confidential. . . .

In addition to overstating its concerns with a suspicion-based program, the District seems to have understated the extent to which such a program is less intrusive of students' privacy. By invading the privacy of a few students rather than many (nationwide, of thousands rather than millions), and by giving potential search targets substantial control over whether they will, in fact, be searched, a suspicion-based scheme is significantly less intrusive. . . .

STUDENTS ARE UNDER CONSTANT SUPERVISION

But having misconstrued the fundamental role of the individualized suspicion requirement in Fourth Amendment analysis, the Court never seriously engages the practicality of such a requirement in the instant case. And that failure is crucial because nowhere is it less clear that an individualized suspicion requirement would be ineffectual than in the school context. In most schools, the entire pool of potential search targets—students—is under constant supervision by teachers and administrators and coaches, be it in classrooms, hallways, or locker rooms.

The record here indicates that the Vernonia schools are no exception. The great irony of this case is that most (though not all) of the evidence the District introduced to justify its suspicionless drug-testing program consisted of first- or second-hand stories of particular, identifiable students acting in ways that plainly gave rise to reasonable suspicion of in-school drug use—and thus that would have justified a drug-related search under our T.L.O. decision. . . .

In light of all this evidence of drug use by particular students, there is a substantial basis for concluding that a vigorous regime of suspicion-based testing (for which the District appears already to have rules in place) would have gone a long way toward solving Vernonia's school drug problem while preserving the Fourth Amendment rights of student athlete/plaintiff James Acton and others like him. And were there any doubt about such a conclusion, it is removed by indications in the record that suspicion-based testing could have been supplemented by an equally vigorous campaign to have Vernonia's parents encourage their children to submit to the District's voluntary drug testing program. In these circumstances, the Fourth Amendment dictates that a mass, suspicionless search regime is categorically unreasonable.

I recognize that a suspicion-based scheme, even where reasonably effective in controlling in-school drug use, may not be as effective as a mass, suspicionless testing regime. In one sense, that is obviously true just as it is obviously true that suspicion-based law enforcement is not as effective as mass, suspicionless enforcement might be. "But," as we stated in *Arizona v. Hicks* (1987), "there is nothing new in the realization" that Fourth Amendment protections come with a price. Indeed, the price we pay is higher in the criminal context, given that police do not closely observe the entire class of potential search targets (all citizens in the area) and must ordinarily adhere to the rigid requirements of a warrant and probable cause.

LENIENCY AND SCHOOL SEARCHES

The principal counterargument to all this, central to the Court's opinion, is that the Fourth Amendment is more lenient with respect to school searches. That is no doubt correct, for, as the Court explains, schools have traditionally had special guardian-like responsibilities for children that necessitate a degree of constitutional leeway. This principle explains the considerable Fourth Amendment leeway we gave school officials in *T.L.O.* In that case, we held that children at school do not enjoy two of the Fourth Amendment's traditional categorical protections against unreasonable searches and seizures: the warrant requirement and the probable cause requirement. And this was true even though the same children enjoy such protections "in a nonschool setting."

The instant case, however, asks whether the Fourth Amendment is even more lenient than that, i.e., whether it is so lenient that students may be deprived of the Fourth Amendment's only remaining, and most basic, categorical protection: its strong preference for an individualized suspicion requirement, with its accompanying antipathy toward personally intrusive, blanket searches of mostly innocent people. It is not at all clear that people in prison lack this categorical protection, and we have said "we are not yet ready to hold that the schools and the prisons need be equated for purposes of the Fourth Amendment." Thus, if we are to mean what we often proclaim—that students do not "shed their constitutional rights . . . at the schoolhouse gate"—the answer must plainly be no.

For the contrary position, the Court relies on cases such as *T.L.O.*, *Ingraham v.Wright* (1977), and *Goss v. Lopez* (1975). But I find the Court's reliance on these cases ironic. If anything, they affirm that schools have substantial constitutional leeway in carrying out their traditional mission of responding to particularized wrongdoing.

By contrast, intrusive, blanket searches of school children, most of whom are innocent, for evidence of serious wrongdoing are not part of any traditional school function of which I am aware. Indeed, many schools, like many parents, prefer to trust their children unless given reason to do otherwise. As James Acton's father said on the witness stand, "[suspicionless testing] sends a message to children that are trying to be responsible citizens . . . that they have to prove that they're innocent . . . , and I think that kind of sets a bad tone."

PHYSICAL EXAMS AND VACCINATIONS

I find unpersuasive the Court's reliance on the widespread practice of physical examinations and vaccinations, which are both blanket searches of a sort. Of course, for these practices to have any Fourth Amendment significance, the Court has to assume that these physical exams and vaccinations are typically "required" to a similar extent that urine testing and collection is required in the instant case, i.e., that they are required regardless of parental objection and that some meaningful sanction attaches to the failure to submit. In any event, without forming any particular view of such searches, it is worth noting that a suspicion requirement for vaccinations is not merely impractical; it is nonsensical, for vaccinations are not searches for anything in particular and so there is nothing about which to be suspicious. Nor is this saying anything new; it is the same theory on which, in part, we have repeatedly upheld certain inventory searches. As for physical examinations, the practicability of a suspicion requirement is highly doubtful because the conditions for which these physical exams ordinarily search, such as latent heart conditions, do not manifest themselves in observable behavior the way school drug use does.

It might also be noted that physical exams (and of course vaccinations) are not searches for conditions that reflect wrongdoing on the part of the student, and so are wholly nonaccusatory and have no consequences that can be regarded as punitive. These facts may explain the absence of Fourth Amendment challenges to such searches. By contrast, although I agree with the Court that the accusatory nature of the District's testing program is diluted by making it a blanket one, any testing program that searches for conditions plainly reflecting serious wrongdoing can never be made wholly nonaccusatory from the student's perspective, the motives for the program notwithstanding; and for the same reason, the substantial consequences that can flow from a positive test, such as suspension from sports, are invariably—and quite reasonably—understood as punishment. The best proof that the District's testing program is to some extent accusatory can be found in James Acton's own explanation on the witness stand as to why he did not want to submit to drug testing: "Because I feel that they have no reason to think I was taking drugs." It is hard to think of a manner of explanation that resonates more intensely in our Fourth Amendment tradition than this.

OTHER FLAWS

I do not believe that suspicionless drug testing is justified on these facts. But even if I agreed that some such testing were reasonable here, I see two other Fourth Amendment flaws in the District's program. First, and most serious, there is virtually no evidence in the record of a drug problem at the Washington Grade School, which includes the 7th and 8th grades, and which Acton attended when this litigation began. This is not surprising, given that, of the four witnesses who testified to drug-related incidents, three were teachers and/or coaches at the high school, and the fourth, though the principal of the grade school at the time of the litigation, had been employed as principal of the high school during the years leading up to (and beyond) the implementation of the drug testing policy. The only evidence of a grade school drug problem that my review of the record uncovered is a "guarantee" by the late-arriving grade school principal that "our problems we've had in '88 and '89 didn't start at the high school level. They started in the elementary school." But I would hope that a single assertion of this sort would not serve as an adequate basis on which to uphold mass, suspicionless drug testing of two entire grades of student athletes—in Vernonia and, by the Court's reasoning, in other school districts as well. Perhaps there is a drug problem at the grade school, but one would not know it from this record. At the least, then, I would insist that the parties and the District Court address this issue on remand.

Second, even as to the high school, I find unreasonable the school's choice of student athletes as the class to subject to suspicionless testing—a choice that appears to have been driven more by a belief in what would pass constitutional muster than by a belief in what was required to meet the District's principal disciplinary concern. Reading the full record in this case, as well as the District Court's authoritative summary of it, it seems quite obvious that the true driving force behind the District's adoption of its drug testing program was the need to combat the rise in drug-related disorder and disruption in its classrooms and around campus. I mean no criticism of the strength of that interest. On the contrary, where the record demonstrates the existence of such a problem, that interest seems self-evidently compelling. Lewis Powell noted in *T.L.O.*, "Without first establishing discipline and maintaining order, teachers cannot begin to educate their students." And the record in this case surely demonstrates there was a drug-related discipline problem in Vernonia of "'epidemic proportions.'" The evidence of a drug-related sports injury problem at Vernonia, by contrast, was considerably weaker.

On this record, then, it seems to me that the far more reasonable choice would have been to focus on the class of students found to have violated published school rules against severe disruption in class and around campus—disruption that had a strong nexus to drug use, as the District established at trial. Such a choice would share two of the virtues of a suspicion-based regime: testing dramatically fewer students, tens as against hundreds, and giving students control, through their behavior, over the likelihood that they would be tested. Moreover, there would be a reduced concern for the accusatory nature of the search, because the Court's feared "badge of shame" would already exist, due to the antecedent accusation and finding of severe disruption. . . .

AN UNREASONABLE SEARCH

It cannot be too often stated that the greatest threats to our constitutional freedoms come in times of crisis. But we must also stay mindful that not all government responses to such times are hysterical overreactions; some crises are quite real, and when they are, they serve precisely as the compelling state interest that we have said may justify a measured intrusion on constitutional rights. The only way for judges to mediate these conflicting impulses is to do what they should do anyway: stay close to the record in each case that appears before them, and make their judgments based on that alone. Having reviewed the record here, I cannot avoid the conclusion that the District's suspicionless policy of testing all student-athletes sweeps too broadly, and too imprecisely, to be reasonable under the Fourth Amendment.

"*According to the U.S. Supreme Court, each and every electronic intercept constitutes a search and seizure under the Fourth Amendment.*"

WIRETAPS VIOLATE THE RIGHT TO PRIVACY

Laura W. Murphy

In 1996, Congress passed two bills that expanded the authority of federal law enforcement officials to perform wiretaps and other forms of electronic surveillance. In the following viewpoint, Laura W. Murphy argues against the passage of these bills. She asserts that wiretaps by the FBI have unnecessarily intercepted millions of innocent conversations. She contends that the FBI is pushing for these bills because it fears that advancing technology may hinder its ability to listen in on private conversations. If these bills are passed, she maintains, the privacy of millions of innocent people will be in jeopardy. Murphy is the director of the national office of the American Civil Liberties Union, an organization that defends civil rights guaranteed by the U.S. Constitution.

As you read, consider the following questions:

1. How many conversations are intercepted by each wiretap or other form of electronic surveillance, according to Murphy?
2. By how much did the number of electronic surveillance intercepts increase between 1984 and 1994, as reported by the author?
3. In Murphy's opinion, why is the FBI's assurance that it will have to receive a court order for electronic surveillance misleading?

Reprinted from Laura W. Murphy, "Congress Plans 'National Wiretap Week,'" on the American Civil Liberties Union Freedom Network at www.aclu.org/news/0327two.html, March 1996, by permission of the American Civil Liberties Union.

There's been no official proclamation, but the U.S. Congress is preparing to celebrate "National Wiretap Week" from March 13th through the 20th, 1996. During this seven-day period, two pieces of legislation—the so-called antiterrorism act and the immigration bill—are scheduled for debate on the floor of the House. Taken together, these bills would dramatically expand federal law enforcement powers, including federal wiretap authority. [Both bills were passed into law in 1996.]

These bills continue the relentless press from Federal law enforcement authorities for wider powers. Yet in a November 1995 letter to the House Judiciary Committee, FBI Director Louis Freeh assured a nervous Congress that his department had no intention of expanding the number of wiretaps or the extent of wiretapping.

DECEPTION

And this is not the only sign of deception. Only two weeks before his November letter, the FBI published a stealthily phrased notice in the Federal Register signaling, in effect, that the federal government wants to require the nation's phone companies to radically alter their critical electronic equipment to enable the Bureau to eavesdrop on one out of every one hundred telephone conversations occurring at any given time in the nation's largest cities and other, undefined prime target areas.

Which FBI should we believe? Is Director Freeh deceiving Congress or does the FBI not understand the full consequences of its own wiretapping proposals and the bills that it supports? From all the evidence, it seems that Director Freeh is trying to hide the truth: the FBI certainly does intend to expand wiretapping, as it has done in each of the years that Mr. Freeh has been at the helm of the agency.

PRIVACY IS AT STAKE

Clearly, what is at stake is our privacy. We must be secure in the knowledge that our government is not turning into Big Brother by eavesdropping on our every conversation. According to the U.S. Supreme Court, each and every electronic intercept constitutes a search and seizure under the Fourth Amendment. Already, too many innocent conversations—nearly two million in 1994 alone—are intercepted by federal and local law enforcement wiretaps. In fact, every time a wiretap or other form of electronic surveillance is placed, nearly 1,000 innocent conversations are intercepted.

According to data from the Administrative Office of the United States Courts, federal law enforcement agencies increasingly use wiretaps and other forms of electronic surveillance. In fact, from 1984 to 1994, the number of federal law enforcement electronic surveillance intercepts nearly doubled. (Electronic surveillance, these days, includes wiretaps, telephone number traces, electronic listening devices commonly known as "bugs," and interception of pager transmissions, E-mail and cellular telephone conversations.)

THE FUTURE IS AT STAKE

And the future, if the FBI has its way, is even more grim. The Clinton Administration's so called counter terrorism legislation—which is being pushed by Director Freeh—would expand the list of felony investigations in which an electronic surveillance order could be sought, expand authority to conduct "roving" wiretaps and wiretaps without a prior court order, and permit the FBI to use the fruits of illegal wiretaps in court when law enforcement officials act illegally but do so in "good faith." Similarly, the immigration legislation would dramatically expand the list of crimes for which a wiretap could be placed.

Although the FBI would have us believe that more wiretapping is needed to save the country from terrorists and prevent another Oklahoma City, the numbers simply do not support the assertion. Though authorized already, wiretapping is almost never used to investigate bombings, arson or firearms violations. Indeed, the last time a wiretap was requested by a law enforcement agency to investigate one of these crimes was in 1988. In the past 11 years, fewer than 0.2 percent of all law enforcement wiretap requests were made in connection with such crimes. Instead 83 percent of all electronic surveillance intercepts are sought to investigate possible gambling and drug offenses.

To assuage the American public, already jittery from exposure of possible federal law enforcement abuses at Waco and Ruby Ridge, the FBI assures us that it will still have to go to court and demonstrate probable cause to a judge before it is allowed to engage in electronic surveillance. What it neglects to mention, however, is that its requests for wiretaps are almost never turned down by the courts: no request for a law enforcement intercept has been rejected since 1988; no request for a foreign intelligence intercept has been turned down since 1979.

The FBI's assurance also fails for another more fundamental reason. In every decade since the Bureau was created, the FBI has engaged in unconstitutional harassment and surveillance of

.2% Arson, bombing, firearms

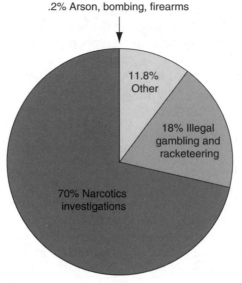

Out of 9,553 electronic surveillance applications filed by federal and state authorities between 1986 and 1996, only 19—less than 0.2 percent—were for investigations concerning arson, bombs, or firearms.

Source: Ira Glasser, "Memo to Congress," August 11, 1996.

disfavored individuals and groups like civil rights activists or peace activists. And if history is any guide, it will not be until 2005 that we learn if this decade's victims may include legal gun owners, non-violent militias or anti-abortion activists.

NEW TECHNOLOGY

Why is this all coming to light now? Why suddenly are we learning of the FBI's seemingly insatiable desire to listen in on our conversations? The answer, in one word, is technology.

As the nation continues its switch from analog to more efficient digital telephone networks, the FBI fears it will lose its ability to wiretap completely. Last year, with that fear in mind, the Justice Department persuaded Congress to pass digital telephony legislation that—for the first time in our history—endorsed the radical notion that the government could require an entire industry to alter its technology so the government could continue to snoop.

The digital telephony legislation, which was bitterly opposed both by privacy advocates and some in the telecommunications industry, is akin to requiring builders to put listening devices in the walls of the new homes they build so the bugs could be turned on one day if the government wants to listen in.

Similarly, in another example of devastatingly bad judgment, the FBI is trying to convince Congress to make it illegal to have a conversation made private through encryption unless the Bureau is given a key so, if it wants to, it can crack the code and listen in. This plan is being bitterly opposed by industry groups and privacy advocates.

In this age of massive commercial databases and computers storing and sorting through every detail of our private lives, it would be nice to think that technological advances could actually improve our privacy rights. But the FBI seems determined, for reasons as yet unknown, to turn this potential benefit against us, thereby stripping more of our constitutional rights.

Instead of turning March 13–20 into "National Wiretapping Week," Congress would be wise to put the brakes on the FBI and take a second look at the proposals it has approved or is considering: the digital telephony legislation, the pending counter-terrorism legislation, and the wiretapping provisions of the immigration bill. The rights protected by our Constitution should be respected every day of the year.

> "Civilized life is a compromise, and wiretaps have proved their value beyond doubt: over the last decade, wiretaps have played a role in convicting tens of thousands of felons."

WIRETAPS ARE NECESSARY TO FIGHT CRIME

David Gelernter

David Gelernter, a computer science professor at Yale University, is a two-time victim of letter bombs sent by the Unabomber, Ted Kaczynski. He is also the author of *The Muse in the Machine* and *Drawing Life*. In the following viewpoint, Gelernter argues that individual privacy must be compromised in the name of safety and security for society. For this reason, he insists, the federal government must be allowed to tap phones when necessary to investigate suspected criminals. However, he adds, improving technology may soon render traditional methods of surveillance obsolete. Therefore, Gelernter contends, it is reasonable to require communications companies to modify their equipment so that the FBI can continue the surveillance that is necessary for the country's safety and protection.

As you read, consider the following questions:

1. According to the author, what is the purpose of the Digital Telephony and Communications Privacy Improvement Act?
2. How does Gelernter respond to critics of the telephony act who charge that the improvements required will be difficult and will not advance their company's competitiveness?
3. In what ways are an individual's right to privacy routinely invaded by the government, according to Gelernter?

I'd be furious if my phone were tapped. Most people would. Americans have a long, proud history of low tolerance for Government snooping. Nonetheless, I strongly support the Government's ability to tap telephones when wiretapping serves a compelling law-enforcement end. Civilized life is a compromise, and wiretaps have proved their value beyond doubt: over the last decade, wiretaps have played a role in convicting tens of thousands of felons and solving (or preventing) large numbers of ghastly crimes. They seem particularly valuable in cases of large-scale drug trafficking and terrorist thuggery.

But in the age of high technology, the wiretap is a dead duck. In the old days, all conversations associated with a given phone number were funneled through one physical pathway, and by spying on that pathway you could hear it all. Nowadays, cellular phones and call forwarding make it much harder to find the right spot and to attach a tap. New techniques coming into use will make it harder still: when many conversations are squished together and sent barreling over a high-capacity glass fiber, it's hard for wiretappers to extract the one conversation they are after from the resulting mush.

THE DIGITAL TELEPHONY AND COMMUNICATIONS PRIVACY IMPROVEMENT ACT

Enter the Administration's Digital Telephony and Communications Privacy Improvement Act. Its goal is to save wiretapping. Congress will act on it soon. It is a good and an important bill. Congress should pass it. [The bill was passed into law in 1994.]

The heart of the act requires phone companies to give law-enforcement agents the ability to execute "all court orders and lawful authorizations for the interception of wire and electronic communications"—whatever fancy new technology happens to be in vogue. It offers the phone companies $500 million to refit telephone equipment to allow compliance with the act. If the costs exceed $500 million, the Administration says, it will seek funds to cover them.

Not everyone is happy with this bill. Some telephone companies argue that the required refitting is technically hard and does nothing for competitiveness or consumer satisfaction. Some civil libertarians argue that the bill poses a threat to privacy.

THE PROBLEMS

The bill does present a wide range of technical problems. In some cases, for example, it requires that the software controlling existing digital switches be modified; the phone companies are right when they argue that these changes would be a first-rate headache to carry out. Nor will the effort advance their competitiveness, or deliver anything exciting to the consumer. But, alas, not every civic duty is fun. And this bill sets a welcome precedent by honestly owning up to the costs and offering to pay them. The message I hope Congress will send to the phone companies is: stop whining and do it.

AN EFFECTIVE TOOL TO FIGHT CRIME

Every day, vicious, murderous criminals use the nation's telephone systems to conduct a diabolical trade in kidnapping, extortion, organized crime, drug trafficking and foreign espionage.

Since 1968, when Congress enacted a formal regime to regulate the use of wiretaps by state and federal law enforcement agencies, numerous crimes have been thwarted or solved and hundreds of thugs and bandits have been jailed.

Henry J. Hyde, *North (San Diego) County Times*, November 17, 1996.

The more troublesome objection deals with privacy. Part of the opposition is based on simple misunderstanding. Some opponents believe that the act will give the Government new spying powers. In fact, the Government will be allowed to do exactly what it has always been allowed to do. The act is intended merely to make it technically possible for law enforcement to continue placing wiretaps.

Other opponents do understand the bill and are forthright about their intentions. If technical advances kill wiretapping, they will send flowers and have a party. They argue that wiretaps aren't terribly useful anyway. This argument is also being advanced in the context of the "clipper chip," another Administration initiative that lives right next door.

THE CLIPPER CHIP

The clipper chip is a small piece of computer hardware designed to stave off encryption schemes that the Government can't crack. The chip would encode all information sent out into any computer network (the Internet, for example) so it can be read only by the intended recipient—and, if necessary, a court-authorized law-enforcement agent who has the key.

Because wiretapping is useless if all you can overhear is gibberish, the Administration would like every computer to come factory-equipped with such a chip. Each chip would have its own key, and the keys would not be handed out like lollipops:

each would be split in two, and each half would be lodged for safekeeping in its own Government vault somewhere.

Of course, the fact that some encryption scheme comes built-in doesn't mean that you have to use it. You can throw out your factory disk drive and plug in another. You could plug in a different Government-proof encryption scheme just as easily. Hence, anti-clipperites gleefully conclude, the chip would be useless for law enforcement, because only a half-wit would discuss a crime using plain vanilla, straight-from-the-factory encryption. And after all, who ever heard of a stupid criminal?

It is impossible to take this kind of argument seriously. What kind of half-wit criminal would leave fingerprints, make calls on any home telephone or return a rental van that played a starring role in a big-budget terrorist spectacular? Many criminals *are* half-wits, many others are lazy or careless, and it's lucky they are. Clipper will make computer-based communication routinely safe and private, in a way that gives us a fighting chance of keeping our ability to spy on criminals. It is no cure-all, but it is a useful and intelligent step.

THE RIGHT TO PRIVACY

Whatever the details, opponents of initiatives like the clipper chip and the telephony act argue that they threaten the right to privacy. But in itself the right to privacy is no argument at all. We allow the Government to violate our privacy routinely for many purposes. The Internal Revenue Service makes a habit of violating it. Search warrants violate it. Privacy buffs are often big fans of gun control and the Endangered Species Act; some versions of gun control restrict the objects you may keep in your own home, and the species act has been interpreted in a way that drastically restricts the ways citizens may use their land. Whether the proposed legislation constitutes a potential invasion of privacy is immaterial. The question is, Is that a justifiable invasion? Experience suggests that it is eminently justifiable.

If Congress fails to pass the telephony bill, there is every reason to believe that crime, particularly terrorist crime, will get worse. And when it happens we will shrug our shoulders, wonder vaguely how things got this way, build more prisons, tend our wounds, bury our dead—as is our wont.

EXPERTS AND COMMON SENSE

All of this suggests a broader moral. A current project of mine involves a detailed study of the 1939 New York World's Fair. One of the questions I face again and again is: Over two generations during which our wealth and technical knowledge and medical expertise have all increased immeasurably, our laws have become more just and our human resources have expanded enormously—how can it be that our confidence in the future has all but collapsed? One part of the answer is that all too often we have allowed experts to come between us and our common sense.

Modern life is so complex that it often feels as if common sense can get no purchase on it. Common sense suggests that this is no time to abandon a useful weapon in the fight on crime. But if telecommunications experts tell us that we just don't understand modern phone systems well enough to make rules about them, if legal experts or would-be experts assure us that for reasons we don't fully understand, if we pass this bill we will regret it . . . who are we to object?

Nothing would do us more good as a nation than to reassert our right to tell the experts to get lost. I am a "technical expert," but don't take my word on this bill as an expert. I was seriously and permanently injured by a terrorist letter bomb in 1993, but don't take my word as a special pleader either. Take my word because common sense demands that wiretapping be preserved. This bill preserves it. Let's pass the bill.

PERIODICAL BIBLIOGRAPHY

The following articles have been selected to supplement the diverse views presented in this chapter. Addresses are provided for periodicals not indexed in the *Readers' Guide to Periodical Literature*, the *Alternative Press Index*, the *Social Sciences Index*, or the *Index to Legal Periodicals and Books*.

Mark Frankel	"Candid Camera," *New Republic,* May 20, 1996.
James Gleick	"Big Brother Is Us," *New York Times Magazine,* September 29, 1996.
David Gollaher	"The Paradox of Genetic Privacy," *New York Times,* January 7, 1998.
Christine Gorman	"Who's Looking at Your Files?" *Time,* May 6, 1996.
David M. Halbfinger	"As Surveillance Cameras Peer, Some Wonder if They Also Pry," *New York Times,* February 22, 1998.
Issues and Controversies On File	"Celebrity Privacy," November 7, 1997. Available from Facts On File, 11 Penn Plaza, New York, NY 10001-2006.
Michael Kinsley	"Orwell Got It Wrong," *Reader's Digest,* June 1997.
Ira A. Lipman	"Drug Testing Is Vital in the Workplace," *USA Today,* January 1995.
Martin London	"There Oughta Be a Law," *George,* November 1997. Available from 30 Montgomery St., Jersey City, NJ 07032.
Jeffrey Rosen	"The End of Privacy," *New Republic,* February 16, 1998.
James Rule and Lawrence Hunter	"Privacy Wrongs," *Washington Monthly,* November 1996.
William Safire	"Nobody's Business," *New York Times,* January 8, 1998.
Patrice Duggan Samuels	"Who's Reading Your E-Mail? Maybe the Boss," *New York Times,* May 12, 1996.
Richard A. Spinello	"The End of Privacy," *America,* January 4, 1997.
D. Van Skilling	"Values, Ethics, and Data About People," *Vital Speeches of the Day,* August 15, 1996.

CHAPTER 3

SHOULD CHURCH AND STATE BE SEPARATE?

Chapter Preface

Despite Supreme Court rulings to the contrary, some areas of the country still start every school day, sporting event, civic meeting, or court day with a prayer. Organized prayers are especially prevalent in the South, where the general population is more supportive of public prayer.

In 1993, the American Civil Liberties Union (ACLU) sued Roy S. Moore, a circuit court judge in Etowah County, Alabama, to stop him from opening his court sessions with a prayer and to force him to remove a plaque of the Ten Commandments from its prominent display in his courtroom. The state-sponsored prayers and religious display violated the separation of church and state, the ACLU argued. Another district court judge agreed in February 1997, ruling that the Ten Commandments plaque was an attempt by Moore to promote religion and therefore was unconstitutional. He stayed his decision, however, pending a ruling by the Alabama Supreme Court.

Moore explains that his refusal to remove the plaque is due to "a higher law that we're bound to recognize" and to the fact that public officials have a duty to "acknowledge the God upon which this nation was founded." He is supported by the Alabama governor, Fob James Jr., who threatened to call out the National Guard and state troopers to protect Moore's display of the Ten Commandments. State attorney general Bill Pryor also backs him, as well as 88 percent of Alabamans surveyed in a November 1997 poll. In January 1998, the Alabama Supreme Court dismissed the case on a technicality, ruling that the ACLU had no legal grounds to bring the lawsuit. The dismissal allows Moore, at least for the present time, to keep his plaque on the wall and to start each court session with a prayer.

Americans are confused over how high the wall should be that separates church and state. They firmly believe in their right to practice religion but also in their right to be free of religion. The authors in the following chapter express different opinions about how separate church and state should be.

"There is no question that the nation's founders meant the First Amendment to disestablish any and all religions from state sponsorship or control."

THE CONSTITUTION'S FRAMERS INTENDED STRICT SEPARATION OF CHURCH AND STATE

Baptist Joint Committee on Public Affairs

The Baptist Joint Committee on Public Affairs (BJC) is a religious organization dedicated to preserving religious liberty and the separation of church and state. In the following viewpoint, the BJC argues that the separation of church and state is necessary for the political health and long life of a nation. The Founding Fathers and religious leaders realized the importance of church-state separation and included it in the First Amendment, the committee asserts. According to the BJC, an examination of the different versions of the First Amendment that did not pass in Congress clearly shows that the framers of the Constitution intended that church and state should remain separate.

As you read, consider the following questions:

1. According to the Baptist committee, what New Testament example supports the practice of separating church and state?
2. What examples does the BJC give to illustrate its contention that cultures decline when church and state are not kept separated?
3. According to the BJC, why is the argument that the Constitution's founders merely intended to prevent the preferential treatment of one religion over another misguided?

Reprinted from the Baptist Joint Committee on Public Affairs, "Separation of Church and State," Life and Liberty series, 1996, by permission.

Religious liberty is a biblical principle and a Baptist distinctive. Because Baptists throughout their history also have advocated separation of church and state, the understandable tendency to equate the two sometimes surfaces. Yet the two—religious liberty and separation of church and state—are not synonyms.

A better way to look at these two related principles is to see separation of church and state as the political corollary to the biblical/theological idea of religious liberty. Why is the distinction between the two important? In part, it is important because although God made every person with free soul and conscience, not all persons enjoy the benefits of a political system that separates the realms of church and state. To say it in another way, all of God's children have souls and consciences that are free under any form of human government, but not all of God's children are blessed to live in societies that keep church and state at a healthy distance from one another.

At the same time, the distinction must not be overdrawn, for the New Testament certainly affirms the idea of separation of church and state, as well as that of religious liberty.

WHAT THE NEW TESTAMENT SAYS

The best known passage on the subject is Matthew 22:15–22, the account of Jesus' interrogation by the Pharisees and Herodians over the lawfulness of paying taxes to the Roman emperor. On the one hand, they hoped Jesus would answer that it was indeed lawful to pay taxes to Caesar so they could accuse him of complicity with the despised Romans. On the other, they wanted him to say it was unlawful to pay taxes so they could accuse him of insurrection. Instead, Jesus disarmed them by replying, "Render therefore to Caesar the things that are Caesar's, and to God the things that are God's" (v. 21). No better formula for the proper relationship between church and state has ever been set forth.

Dr. George W. Truett, a former Southern Baptist Convention President, in his famous sermon on religious liberty at the U.S. Capitol in 1920, commented on this incident:

> That utterance of Jesus, "Render therefore unto Caesar the things that which are Caesar's, and unto God the things that are God's," is one of the most revolutionary and history-making utterances that ever fell from those lips divine. That utterance, once and for all, marked the divorcement of church and state. It marked a new era for the creeds and deeds of men. It was the sunrise gun of a new day, the echoes of which are to go on and on and on until in every land, whether great or small, the doctrine shall have absolute supremacy everywhere of a free church in a free state.

GOD OR COUNTRY?

One of the classic dilemmas for Christians always has been the choice between God and country. For while sometimes Christians can affirm both, at other times they are forced to choose between the two. Nowhere in the New Testament is the dilemma more clearly presented than in Peter and John's choice between preaching about Jesus or following orders to cease doing so (see Acts 4–5). When first ordered to stop preaching, they replied, "Whether it be right in the sight of God to hearken unto you more than unto God, judge ye. For we cannot but speak the things which we have seen and heard" (Acts 4:19–20). After performing many signs and wonders, Peter and John were arrested and, when brought before the council, were reminded of the order. This time they answered, "We must obey God rather than men" (Acts 5:29).

The clear command of the New Testament is that allegiance to God is demanded when challenged by obedience to the powers of this world. In his letter to the Philippians, Paul reminded them: "But our commonwealth is in heaven, and from it we await a Savior, the Lord Jesus Christ" (Philippians 3:20). Early in the fifth century A.D., Augustine of Hippo wrote a classic treatise contrasting the Christian's loyalty to God and to country. In *The City of God*, he set forth the idea that the Christian's primary citizenship rests in heaven and his citizenship in any earthly realm is only secondary. Christians of every age need to remember those priorities.

Addressing this very matter, Dr. Truett, at a dramatic moment in his U.S. Capitol address, declared:

> In behalf of our Baptist people I am compelled to say that forgetfulness of the[se] principles . . . explains many of the religious ills that now afflict the world. All went well with the early churches in their earlier days. They were incomparably triumphant days for the Christian faith. Those early disciples of Jesus, without prestige and worldly power, yet aflame with the love and God and the passion of Christ, went out and shook the pagan Roman Empire from center to circumference, even in one brief generation. Christ's religion needs no prop of any kind from any worldly source, and to the degree that it is thus supported is a millstone hanged about its neck.

Dr. Truett was right. As long as the followers of Christ depended on nothing more than the power of God to expand Christ's kingdom all went well.

But in what must be called one of the most tragic moves ever made by an earthly ruler, the emperor Constantine (d. 337) declared Rome to be a Christian empire, throwing the weight of his position behind Christianity. With that fusing of the empire to the church, both began a long decline that resulted eventually in the domination of the empire by the church. That union of church and state further resulted in holy wars and inquisitions in a time so bleak it came to be known as the Dark Ages.

PROTECTING BOTH RELIGION AND GOVERNMENT

Thomas Jefferson and James Madison held an expansive view of the First Amendment, arguing that church-state separation would protect both religion and government.

Madison specifically feared that a small group of powerful churches would join together and seek establishment or special favors from the government. To prevent this from happening, Madison spoke of the desirability of a "multiplicity of sects" that would guard against government favoritism.

Jefferson and Madison did not see church-state separation as an "either or" proposition or argue that one institution needed greater protection than the other. As historian Garry Wills points out in his 1990 book *Under God*, Jefferson believed that no worthy religion would seek the power of the state to coerce belief. In his notes he argued that disestablishment would strengthen religion, holding that it would "oblige its ministers to be industrious [and] exemplary." The state likewise was degraded by an established faith, Jefferson asserted, because establishment made it a partner in a system based on bribery of religion.

Madison also argued that establishment was no friend to religion or the state. He insisted that civil society would be hindered by establishment, charging that attempts to enforce religious belief by law would weaken government. In his 1785 *Memorial and Remonstrance*, Madison stated flatly that "Religion is not helped by establishment, but is hurt by it."

Americans United for Separation of Church and State, *Eleven Myths About Church and State*, 1996.

While the Protestant Reformation broke the Holy Roman Empire, it did not result in the dissolution of church-state ties. In Germany, Luther advocated church-state union, while in Geneva, John Calvin established his own "holy city." In England, after King Henry VIII was excommunicated from the Roman Catholic Church over the question of his divorce, he took the Anglican Church with him and declared himself its head.

Only the Anabaptist wing of the Reformation declared a divorce between church and state. It was in Holland where some

English Baptists first learned of this radical "new" way from Anabaptists. When they returned to England, they too advocated separation of church and state.

Yet it was left for America to enshrine the separation of church and state as a national doctrine. Even here, however, the victory for separation was achieved only after a fierce battle. One of the most persistent myths about American history is that English Pilgrims and Puritans quickly established full religious freedom and succeeded immediately in separating church from state on the shores of Massachusetts and Virginia. Nothing could be further from the truth.

Indeed the battle for separation raged for more than 150 years before the principle was enshrined in the national Constitution in 1791 as the cornerstone of the Bill of Rights. Separation of church and state and full religious freedom effectively were guaranteed by the adoption of the First Amendment to the Constitution, which begins with the ringing declaration that "Congress shall make no law respecting an establishment of religion, or prohibiting the free exercise thereof." The other precious First Amendment guarantees are premised on and follow those two: freedom of speech and press and the right to assemble peaceably and redress grievances to the government.

Baptists must not forget it was their denominational forebears who lifted high the torch of a free church in a free state. Indeed it is no exaggeration to say that without the agitation by Baptists over what they saw as the proper relationship between church and state, the final victory would not have been won.

Although many Baptist leaders and ordinary laypeople were directly involved in that determined struggle, three stand out. More than any other individuals in colonial America, these three deserve the eternal gratitude of Baptists and all other Americans for forging the basic arrangement separating church and state.

ROGER WILLIAMS

Roger Williams (c. 1603–1683) has been praised by American historians as possessing one of the finest minds among colonists. Yet he was a restless individual who fiercely prized his individuality and that of everybody else. He was a Baptist only briefly— later becoming a self-described "Seeker"—but in that short time made an indelible impression on Baptist history in this country.

Because the Massachusetts Bay Colony had established Congregationalism as the state church and put up barriers of all kinds to anyone not belonging to that church, Williams protested. When he persisted, he was driven from Massachusetts and in exile established Providence Plantation, in what became Rhode Island. There Williams and his hardy band of dissenters organized the first Baptist church on American soil, the First Baptist Church of Providence.

Although some have seen Williams as something of a secularist because of his renunciation of the institutional church, he actually demanded separation of church and state on deeply held theological grounds. He insisted on what he called "soul liberty," a biblical principle that for Williams meant no civil authority should be given jurisdiction over matters of the soul. Thus, he believed civil authorities should have no jurisdiction over churches nor should the church expect support from the authorities.

One can hardly exaggerate the revolutionary nature of such views during the period in which Williams lived. He died a century before his view of separation of church and state was achieved fully. Its achievement in the late 18th century is owed largely to two other Baptist heroes.

ISAAC BACKUS

Isaac Backus (1724–1806) was a Baptist preacher who became an influential figure during the Philadelphia meeting of the Constitutional Congress, the body that declared independence from England and set the basic framework for the new nation. Backus, also of Massachusetts, lobbied the delegation from his colony for the inclusion of a bill of rights that would guarantee the right to free exercise of religion and the right of the church to be free from state's control.

But while his efforts in Philadelphia to change the Massachusetts delegates' minds largely were unsuccessful, Backus found receptive ears among his fellow Baptists. He rallied them to the cause of separation of church and state by traveling thousands of miles on horseback, visiting in their homes and preaching in their churches. He was indeed the most influential Baptist of his generation in America.

Backus lived long enough to see the Bill of Rights incorporated into the new federal Constitution, in no small measure because of his persistent efforts on its behalf. But he died long before his own Massachusetts became the last of the former colonies to disestablish its own church in 1833.

JOHN LELAND

John Leland (1754–1841), like Backus and Williams, began his ministry in Massachusetts, but migrated to Virginia, where he became a key figure in the battle for the Bill of Rights. His is among those names in the Old Dominion state that forever are inscribed on the Baptist honor roll. Leland and other Virginia Baptists steadfastly refused to be regulated by Virginia's colonial authorities who gave preeminence to the Anglican Church as the established religion in the colony.

Leland is best known for his influence on fellow Virginians Thomas Jefferson and James Madison, who became the father of the U.S. Constitution. Leland, in the best sense of the word, lobbied for inclusion of a provision in the federal Bill of Rights to guarantee religious freedom and separation of church and state. His success in convincing Madison of the wisdom of such an arrangement is one of the truly thrilling chapters in Baptist history in this country.

When the original draft of the Constitution was sent to the colonies for ratification, Leland put himself up as a candidate to the Virginia Constitutional Convention. He was opposed by Madison, a neighboring farmer in Orange County. Madison at the time favored ratification of the document as then written, while Leland campaigned on the proposition that it should be rejected because it contained no specific guarantees for religious liberty and other personal freedoms. After a now-famous meeting between the two men, Leland withdrew as a candidate when Madison promised to support a Bill of Rights that would include the guarantees of religious freedom and separation of church and state.

Madison was so convinced by Leland's arguments that he went on to become the principal author of the Bill of Rights, which begins with guarantees of separation of church and state and free exercise of religion.

Unlike either Williams or Backus, Leland lived to see the day when his trailblazing efforts succeeded fully with ratification of the Constitution, including the Bill of Rights, and the disestablishment of state religions in all the colonies.

THE FRAGILE NATURE OF FREEDOM

Despite the heroic efforts of Williams, Backus, Leland and all their Baptist contemporaries who espoused what was then a radical departure from all previous church-state arrangements, religious liberty and separation of church and state are fragile blessings to be both cherished and preserved. The patriot Wendell Phillips declared that "eternal vigilance is the price of liberty."

He was right. Thus present-day Baptists are bound by their own history and, more important, by the faith "once delivered to the saints" to contend for it today.

Remembering that heritage has become increasingly important in recent years as the idea of separation of church and state has come under attack. Some well-known television preachers, for example, deny that the nation's founders intended for church and state to be separate. Some say the Constitution nowhere mentions separation of church and state.

But saying that is like saying the New Testament denies the idea of the Trinity because nowhere does the word appear in the sacred text. Although they knew church and state would interact with each other, they fully intended to keep a creative tension between the two.

The argument has been advanced recently that all the founders intended to accomplish with the First Amendment's religion clauses was to prevent the preferential treatment of one religion over another. Yet an examination of the Philadelphia debate surrounding adoption of the First Amendment puts that contention to rest. In 1789, on the first day of debate on the First Amendment, a motion was made to strike the words "religion, or prohibiting the free exercise thereof" and insert instead "one religious sect or society in preference to others." The motion was defeated.

A second motion was made to strike the amendment altogether. It too was defeated. Yet another motion was made to adopt alternative language: "Congress shall not make any law infringing the rights of conscience, or establishing any religious sect or society." It too was defeated. A fourth motion was made to amend the amendment to read, "Congress shall make no law establishing any particular denomination of religion in preference to another, or prohibiting the free exercise thereof, nor shall the rights of conscience be infringed." Like the others, it too was defeated.

In short, there is no question that the nation's founders meant the First Amendment to disestablish any and all religions from state sponsorship or control and to guarantee the free exercise of religion for all citizens.

"The aim [of the First Amendment]
was to prevent Congress from
establishing a 'national' religion that
would threaten the religious
diversity of the states."

THE CONSTITUTION'S FRAMERS DID NOT INTEND STRICT SEPARATION OF CHURCH AND STATE

M. Stanton Evans

In the following viewpoint, M. Stanton Evans asserts that when the Constitution was written, religion was an important part of people's public and private lives. He argues that the framers of the Constitution did not intend to erect a wall completely separating church and state, as is commonly believed. The First Amendment was merely a safeguard, he contends, against the federal government's establishment of a national religion. Evans is the director of the National Journalism Center in Washington, D.C., and the author of *The Theme Is Freedom: Religion, Politics, and the American Tradition*, from which this viewpoint is adapted.

As you read, consider the following questions:

1. According to Evans, how many colonies had established an official church?
2. In what ways did the states support established religions at the time of the Constitutional Convention, according to Evans?
3. What evidence does the author present to support his contention that the federal government did not prohibit officially sponsored prayer in the nation's early days?

A s the renewed debate over prayer in the public schools suggests, the cultural conflict of the modern era finds vivid and
enduring focus in the legal dispute about the place of religion
in the civic order. Here the battle is overt, relentless, and pervasive—with traditional belief and custom retreating before a secularist onslaught in our courts and other public institutions.

THE SUPREME COURT'S RULINGS

Since the 1960s, the U.S. Supreme Court has handed down a series of rulings that decree a "wall of separation" between affairs
of state and the precepts of religion. In the most controverted of
these cases, in 1962, the Court said an officially sponsored
prayer recited in the New York public schools was an abridge-
ment of our freedoms. This prayer read, in its entirety: "Almighty
God, we acknowledge our dependence on Thee, and we beg Thy
blessings upon us, our parents, our teachers, and our country."
In the Court's opinion, this supplication triggered the First
Amendment ban against an "establishment of religion," logic
that was later extended to reading the Bible and reciting the
Lord's Prayer in the classroom.

In adopting the First Amendment, according to the Court, the
Founders meant to sever all connection between religious faith
and government, requiring that religion be a purely private matter. As Justice Hugo Black put it in an oft-quoted statement: "The
'establishment of religion' clause of the First Amendment means
at least this: Neither a state nor the Federal Government can set
up a church. Neither can pass laws which aid one religion, aid
all religions, or prefer one religion over another. . . . No tax in
any amount, large or small, can be levied to support any religious activities or institutions, whatever they may be called, or
whatever form they may adopt to teach or practice religion."

This doctrine has been affirmed and amplified in many rulings
since. In support of it, Black and his successors (most recently Justice David Souter) have offered a reading of our history that supposedly shows the intentions of the people who devised the First
Amendment. In a nutshell, we're told that the Founders chiefly responsible for the Constitution's religion clauses were James Madison and Thomas Jefferson; that they held views intensely hostile
toward any governmental backing for religion; and that the
amendment was a triumph for their separationist position.

OF WHOLE CLOTH

The First Amendment depicted by Justice Black and other liberal
jurists is a fabrication. The Supreme Court's alleged history is a

prime example of picking and choosing elements from the past to suit the ideological fashions of the present. If we consult the history of the nation's founding, we find that the Court and its supporters have misstated the material facts about the issue in every possible fashion.

To begin with, state papers, legal arrangements, and political comment of the founding generation show that American culture in that period was suffused with religious doctrine. The point is made by the very concept of an "establishment of religion." This term had a definite meaning in England and the colonies that is critical to understanding the debate about the First Amendment. It signified an official church that occupied a privileged position with the state, was vested with certain powers denied to others, and was supported from the public treasury. Such was the Church of England in Great Britain, and such also were numerous churches in the colonies at the beginning of our revolution.

THE STATES' CHURCHES

In 1775, no fewer than nine colonies had such arrangements. Massachusetts, Connecticut, and New Hampshire had systems of local church establishment in favor of the Congregationalists. In the South, from Maryland on down, the establishments were Episcopal. In New York, there was a system of locally supported Protestant clergy. Because of growing religious diversity within the states, pressure mounted to disestablish these official churches. In particular, increasingly numerous Baptists and Presbyterians made headway against the Anglican position, which was further weakened by the identification of many Episcopal ministers with the English.

Even so, at the time of the Constitutional Convention, the three New England states still had their Congregational establishments. In other states, there remained a network of official sanctions for religious belief, principally the requirement that one profess a certain kind of Christian doctrine to hold public office or enjoy other legal privilege. With local variations, these generally tended in the same direction, and they make instructive reading alongside the statements of Justices Black and Souter about the supposed history of our institutions.

In South Carolina, for example, the Constitution of 1778 said that "the Christian Protestant religion shall be deemed . . . the established religion of the state." It further said that no religious society could be considered a church unless it agreed "that there is one eternal God and a future state of rewards and punishment; that the Christian religion is the true religion; that the Holy Scriptures of the Old and New Testaments are of divine inspiration." South Carolina also asserted that "no person who denies the existence of a Supreme Being shall hold any office under this Constitution."

Similar statements can be gleaned from other state enactments of the period. The Maryland Constitution of 1776 decreed, for instance, "a general and equal tax for the support of the Christian religion." New Jersey that year expressed its idea of toleration by saying that "no Protestant inhabitant of this colony shall be denied the enjoyment of any civil right." Massachusetts, in 1780, authorized a special levy to support "public Protestant teachers of piety, religion and morality"—a formula adopted verbatim by New Hampshire.

OFFICIAL SUPPORT FOR RELIGION CONTINUES

Official support for religious faith and state religious requirements for public office persisted well after adoption of the First Amendment. The established church of Massachusetts was not abolished until 1833. In New Hampshire, the requirement that one had to be Protestant to serve in the legislature was continued until 1877. In New Jersey, Roman Catholics were not permitted to hold office until 1844. In Maryland, the stipulation that one had to be a Christian lasted until 1826. As late as 1835, one had to be a Protestant to take office in North Carolina; until 1868, the requirement was that one had to be a Christian; thereafter that one had to profess a belief in God.

The official sanction for religious belief provided by the states was equally apparent at the federal level, during and after the Revolution. Appeals for divine assistance, days of prayer and fasting, and other religious observances were common in the Continental Congress. Among its first items of business, in 1774, the Congress decided to appoint a chaplain and open its proceedings with a prayer. When it was objected that this might be a problem because of diversity in religious doctrine, Sam Adams answered: "I am not a bigot. I can hear a prayer from a man of piety and virtue, who is at the same time a friend of his country."

On June 12, 1775, the Congress called for "a day of public humiliation, fasting, and prayer," wherein "[we] offer up our joint supplications to the all-wise, omnipotent, and merciful disposer of all events." In observance of this fast day, Congress attended an Anglican service in the morning and a Presbyterian service in the afternoon.

During the Revolutionary War, Congress made provision for

military chaplains, recommended that officers and men attend religious service, and threatened court martial for anyone who misbehaved on such occasions. It also adopted the Northwest Ordinance, stressing the need for "religion and morality," appropriated money for the Christian education of Indians, and encouraged the printing of a Bible. The Northwest Ordinance and the measures regarding chaplains, official prayer, and education of the Indians, were re-adopted by the first Congress under the new Constitution and maintained for many years thereafter.

CRUMBLING WALL

Such was the body of doctrine and official practice that surrounded the First Amendment—immediately predating it, adopted while it was being discussed and voted on, and enduring long after it was on the books. The resulting picture is very different from any notion of America as a country run by secularists and Deists. Nor does it look very much like a country in which the governing powers were intent on creating a "wall of separation" between church and state, denying official support to the precepts of religion.

This was the background to Madison's motion on June 8, 1789, introducing a set of amendments to the Constitution, culled from the proposals of the state conventions. Among the measures that he offered was this pertaining to an "establishment of religion": "The civil rights of none shall be abridged on account of religious belief, nor shall any national religion be established . . ." In view of the weight that has been given to Madison's personal opinions on the subject, his comments on this occasion are of special interest. For example, challenged by Roger Sherman as to why such guarantees were needed, given the doctrine of "enumerated powers," Madison said

> he apprehended the meaning of the words to be, that Congress shall not establish a religion and enforce the legal observation of it by law, nor compel men to worship God in any manner contrary to their conscience. Whether the words are necessary or not, he did not mean to say, but they had been required by some of the state conventions, who seemed to entertain an opinion that [under the "necessary and proper" clause] . . . Congress . . . might infringe the rights of conscience and establish a national religion; to prevent these effects he presumed the amendment was intended, and he thought it as well expressed as the nature of language would admit. [Italics added.]

In this and other exchanges, the House debate made two things clear about the Bill of Rights and its religion clauses: 1) Madison was introducing the amendments not because he thought they were needed but because others did, and because he had promised to act according to their wishes; 2) the aim was to prevent *Congress* from establishing a "national" religion that would threaten the religious diversity of the states. Given the varied practices we have noted, ranging from establishments and doctrinal requirements for public office to relative toleration, any "national" religion would have been a source of angry discord.

Reprinted by permission of Chuck Asay and Creators Syndicate.

Against that backdrop, the meaning of the establishment clause as it came out of conference should be crystal clear: "Congress shall make no law respecting an establishment of religion." The agency prohibited from acting is the national legislature; what it is prevented from doing is passing any law "*respecting*" an establishment of religion. In other words, Congress was forbidden to legislate at all concerning church establishment—either for or against. It was prevented from setting up a national established church; equally to the point, *it was prevented from interfering with the established churches in the states.*

Shield Becomes Sword

Though this history is blurred or ignored, it is no secret, and its general features are sometimes acknowledged by liberal spokesmen. It may be conceded, for example, that the First Amendment was intended to be a prohibition against the *Federal* Government. But that guarantee was supposedly broadened by the Fourteenth Amendment, which "applied" the Bill of Rights against the states. Thus what was once prohibited only to the Federal Government is now also prohibited to the states.

Thus we have the Orwellian concept of "applying" a protection of the states *as a weapon against them*—using the First Amendment to achieve the very thing it was intended to prevent. The legitimacy of this reversal has been convincingly challenged by Raoul Berger, Lino Graglia, and James McClellan. But for present purposes, let us simply *assume* the First Amendment restrictions on Congress were "applied" against the states. What then? What did this prohibit?

One thing we know for sure is that it *did not prohibit officially sponsored prayer.* As we have seen, Congress itself engaged in officially sponsored, tax-supported prayer, complete with paid official chaplains, from the very outset—and continues to do so to this day. Indeed, in one of the greatest ironies of this historical record, we see the practice closely linked with passage of the First Amendment—supplying a refutation of the Court's position that is as definitive as could be wished.

A NATIONAL DAY OF PRAYER

The language that had been debated off and on throughout the summer and then hammered out in conference finally passed the House of Representatives on September 24, 1789. *On the very next day,* the self-same House of Representatives passed a resolution calling for *a day of national prayer and thanksgiving.* Here is the language the House adopted: "We acknowledge with grateful hearts the many signal favors of Almighty God, especially by affording them an opportunity peacefully to establish a constitutional government for their safety and happiness."

The House accordingly called on President Washington to issue a proclamation designating a national day of prayer and thanksgiving (the origin of our current legal holiday). This was Washington's response:

> It is the duty of all nations to acknowledge the providence of Almighty God, to obey His will, to be grateful for His benefits, and humbly to implore His protection and favor. . . . That great and glorious Being who is the beneficent author of all the good that was, that is, or that ever will be, that we may then unite in rendering unto Him our sincere and humble thanks for His kind care and protection of the people.

Such were the official sentiments of Congress and the President immediately after adoption of the First Amendment. These statements are far more doctrinal and emphatic than the modest prayer schoolchildren are forbidden to recite because it allegedly violates the First Amendment. If we accept the reasoning of the modern Court, as Robert Cord observes, both *Congress and George Washington violated the intended meaning of the First Amendment from its inception.*

The more logical conclusion, of course, is that Congress knew much better what it meant by the language adopted the preceding day than does our self-consciously evolving Court two centuries later. And in the view of Congress, there was nothing either in law or in logic to bar it from engaging in officially sponsored, tax-supported prayer, then or ever. It follows that the amendment can't possibly bar the states from doing likewise.

MADISON AND JEFFERSON

To all this, the liberal answer is, essentially: James Madison. Whatever the legislative history, we are informed, Madison in his subsequent writings took doctrinaire positions on church-state separation, and these should be read into the First Amendment. This, however, gets the matter topsy-turvy. Clearly, if the Congress that passed the First Amendment, and the states that ratified it, didn't agree with Madison's more stringent private notions, as they surely didn't, then these were *not* enacted. It is the common understanding of the relevant parties, not the ideas of a single individual, especially those expressed in other settings, that defines the purpose of a law or constitutional proviso.

Furthermore, the Court's obsession with the individual views of Madison is highly suspect. It contrasts strangely with judicial treatment of his disclaimers in the House debate, and of his opinion on other constitutional matters. Madison held strict constructionist views on the extent of federal power, arguing that the Constitution reserved undelegated authority to the states. *These* views of Madison are dismissed entirely by the Court. Thus we get a curious inversion: Madison becomes the Court's authority on the First Amendment, even though the notions he later voiced about this subject were not endorsed by others involved in its adoption. On the other hand, he isn't cited on the residual powers of the states, even though his statements on this topic were fully endorsed by other supporters of the Constitution and relied on by the people who voted its approval. It is hard to find a thread of consistency in this—beyond the obvious one of serving liberal ideology.

JEFFERSON'S VIEWS

As peculiar as the Court's selective use of Madison is its resort to Jefferson. The anomaly here is that Jefferson was not a member of the Constitutional Convention, or of the Congress that considered the Bill of Rights, or of the Virginia ratifying convention. But he had strongly separationist views (up to a point) and had worked with Madison for disestablishment and religious freedom in Virginia. For the Court, this proves the First Amendment embodied Jefferson's statement in 1802, in a letter to the Baptists of Connecticut, about a "wall of separation."

Again we pass over the Lewis Carroll logic—in this case deducing the intent of an amendment adopted in 1789 from a letter written 13 years later by a person who had no official role in its adoption. Rather than dwelling on this oddity, we shall simply go to the record and see what Jefferson actually said about the First Amendment and its religion clauses. In his second inaugural address, for example, he said:

> In matters of religion, I have considered that its free exercise is placed by the Constitution independent of the powers of the general government. I have therefore undertaken on no occasion to prescribe the religious exercises suited to it. But I have left them as the Constitution found them, under the direction or discipline of state or church authorities acknowledged by the several religious societies.

Jefferson made the same point a few years later to a Presbyterian clergyman, who inquired about his attitude toward Thanksgiving proclamations:

> I consider the government of the United States as interdicted from intermeddling with religious institutions, their doctrines, discipline, or exercises. This results from the provision that no law shall be made respecting the establishment of religion or the free exercise thereof, but also from that which reserves to the states the powers not delegated to the United States. Certainly no power over religious discipline has been delegated to the general government. It must thus rest with the states as far as it can be in any human authority.

The irresistible conclusion is that there was no wall of separation between religious affirmation and civil government in the several states, nor could the First Amendment, with or without the Fourteenth Amendment, have been intended to create one. The wall of separation, instead, was between the Federal Government and the states, meant to make sure the central authority didn't meddle with the customs of local jurisdictions.

As a matter of constitutional law, the Court's position in these religion cases is an intellectual shambles—results-oriented jurisprudence at its most flagrant. An even greater scandal is the extent to which the Justices have rewritten the official record to support a preconceived conclusion: a performance worthy of regimes in which history is tailored to the interests of the ruling powers. In point of fact, America's constitutional settlement—up to and including the First Amendment—was the work of people who believed in God, and who expressed their faith as a matter of course in public prayer and other governmental practice.

| *"We need kids spending their time in school reading and writing and doing math, not mumbling prayers."*

SCHOOL PRAYER THREATENS RELIGIOUS LIBERTY

Roger Simon

Students do not need a constitutional amendment to be allowed to pray in schools, argues Roger Simon in the following viewpoint. If school prayer is allowed, he contends, the government will dictate what prayers should be said in schools, violating the rights of those whose beliefs are different from the majority. Furthermore, Simon asserts, praying in school will not improve the character of the students who pray. Simon is a syndicated columnist.

As you read, consider the following questions:

1. Who does Simon hold up as proof that public prayers do not improve a person's morals?
2. What is the author's philosophy on how to become a better person?
3. If public prayers were permitted in schools, how would schools decide which prayers to recite, according to Simon?

School prayer goes on every day in America, usually right before a test.

Kids can pray any time they please.

They can pray silently; they can pray out loud (as long as it doesn't disturb the class); they can pray in the halls, in gym and at lunch.

What is now being talked about, however, is a constitutional amendment to create state-sanctioned prayer in the public schools.

Why do we need this?

Because conservative Christians believe that prayer will make kids better students and better people.

To which I say: God hclp us.

LIMITED POWERS

I do not deny the power of prayer. But standing up at the beginning of each day and mumbling words—which is what will happen in the schools—will not make you a better person.

Jim Bakker prayed all the time. So did Jimmy Swaggart. Loudly. And on television. Did it make them better?

The vast majority of priests in this country are good and holy men. But those small number of priests who are child molesters were not transformed by the prayers they said each day.

God not only hears what you say, but I believe, He also looks into your heart. And the mere recitation of prayer is not going to impress Him.

Nor will it make our schools better. A few lightning bolts might help, or maybe another Great Flood, but prayer? Come on.

KIDS NEED TO STUDY

We have not had so useless a debate in America since Congress got all hot and bothered about an amendment to ban flag burning.

We need kids spending their time in school reading and writing and doing math, not mumbling prayers.

I grew up in a household where prayers were said out loud each week. But I was also taught that God helps those who help themselves.

We don't need to teach kids that all they need do is pray in school to make themselves better.

We need to teach them to get educated and work hard.

And if they want to pray, too, that's great. They can do that whenever they want.

But the power of the state should not be used to make prayer official.

And don't kid yourself that those behind this movement want a moment of silence or some nice non-sectarian prayer that all religions can share.

That is not what they want.

A spokesman for the speaker of the House, Newt Gingrich, told *The Washington Post*: "I think we are looking at voluntary school prayer. Not voluntary silence."

Reprinted by permission of Mike Luckovich and Creators Syndicate.

And what kind of prayer will be conducted in the schools?

One of the leading advocates for school prayer in America is Texas minister David Barton.

He has written a book arguing that the Supreme Court's ban on school prayer has led to an increase in violent crime, divorce and teen pregnancy and a drop in student scores on the Scholastic Aptitude Test.

WHAT THE MINORITY CAN EXPECT

What kind of prayer does Barton want in the schools to correct all these things?

Each school district would vote.

And if a majority voted for a Christian prayer or mandatory Bible classes, that is what everyone in the school district would have to accept.

What about Jews or Moslems or Hindus or other non-Christians? (To say nothing of atheists and agnostics.)

Their only recourse, Barton says, would be to persuade the Christian majority to change its vote.

Otherwise, the non-Christians would just have to tolerate the Bible classes and the prayers.

"On any issue, you will always have a group that has its rights violated," Barton says. "If the vote is 98-2, then the two shouldn't win in this country."

And since America is an overwhelmingly Christian country, we can anticipate that Christians will "win" in an overwhelming number of school districts.

This is the America Barton wants. A Christian America. An America where the majority is allowed to impose its will on the minority. Because, as he says, a minority should expect to have "its rights violated."

That's the bad news. The good news is that if Barton is correct, the recitation of prayer will make people smarter, more law-abiding and more moral.

But in Washington, our senators and representatives begin each day with a prayer.

And it hasn't done much for them.

"For the first half of the twentieth
century and all of the nineteenth,
children prayed in school. . . . The
minds of these children were not
destroyed or perverted by these
exposures."

PROHIBITING SCHOOL PRAYER
THREATENS RELIGIOUS LIBERTY

Linda Bowles

According to syndicated columnist Linda Bowles, a vast majority
of parents favor public prayers in school. She maintains that
school prayer was allowed in past generations, posing no threat to
America's government. Children should be able to acknowledge
in school the same divine power that is mentioned in almost all
of the state constitutions, she asserts. Denying students the opportunity to participate in nonsectarian, voluntary prayers at schools
and school events stigmatizes religion, Bowles contends.

As you read, consider the following questions:

1. What percentage of the American public favors school prayer,
   according to a poll cited by Bowles?
2. In the author's opinion, what was the founders' intention for
   the First Amendment?
3. What is Harry V. Jaffa's idea to restore school prayer,
   according to Bowles?

Reprinted from Linda Bowles, "Children Don't Need Protection from Religion,"
Conservative Chronicle, June 26, 1996, by permission of Creators Syndicate. Copyright 1996
Creators Syndicate.

A 1996 Gallup poll confirms the findings of previous polls that school prayer is favored by 70 percent to 75 percent of the public. But with increasing frequency, America's bureaucratic overlords dismiss the will of the people as irrelevant.

WHO PROTECTS THE MAJORITY FROM THE MINORITY?

On June 3, 1996, U.S. District Court Judge Neal Biggers ruled it unconstitutional for a rural Mississippi school to permit morning prayer over the intercom. He said, "The Bill of Rights was created to protect the minority from tyranny by the majority." That raises a question: Who protects the majority from the tyranny of an opinionated judge?

A few days earlier, Florida Gov. Lawton Chiles vetoed an education bill that would have permitted school districts to authorize non-sectarian, voluntary, student-led prayer at graduations and other gatherings such as sports events. Gov. Chiles said, "I do not believe that the right to petition the divine should be granted or withheld by majority vote." That raises a question: Who protects the majority from the tyranny of an opinionated governor?

Regarding church and state, the Constitution simply says that Congress "shall make no law respecting an establishment of religion or prohibiting the free exercise thereof."

It requires tortured reasoning to use this hands-off language to support heavyhanded, judicial tyranny over the rights of the majority and to justify laws that censor religious speech in government schools, prohibit prayer at graduation ceremonies and ban menorahs and nativity scenes at the courthouse.

The founders were trying to protect people from a state-mandated religion; they were not trying to impose secular humanism, or New Age idolatry, as a mandatory system of unbelief.

For the first half of the twentieth century and all of the nineteenth, children prayed in school, read scriptures, sang carols and were able to view the Ten Commandments posted on bulletin boards. The minds of these children were not destroyed or perverted by these exposures, and America was never in any danger of becoming a theocracy.

A SIGNIFICANT CHANGE

Nevertheless, that sensible arrangement changed in 1962 when ideologically impelled members of the Supreme Court ruled that school prayer violates the Constitution. That ruling significantly changed the culture of government schools.

Children are not stupid. They understand that God and all

signs of him have been outlawed from their school. They understand they don't need protection from that which is good for them.

This culture of religious apartheid in government schools inevitably and obviously stigmatizes religion and discredits its messages. It is a culture of active godlessness, one consistent with a curriculum of condoms, alternative lifestyles, relative values and statism. Government schools are not value-neutral.

THE AUTHORITY OF STATE CONSTITUTIONS

Congress has the constitutional authority to immediately pass legislation allowing voluntary prayer in schools. The character of this prayer would be guided by the acknowledgement of God expressed in the preambles of 46 U.S. state constitutions. This would at once recall the idea of "liberty under God," and remind all Americans that acknowledging God has not been a danger to, but rather the formation of our unparalleled freedoms for two centuries.

Larry P. Arnn, in *Emancipating School Prayer*, Harry V. Jaffa, ed., 1996.

There is hope. Harry V. Jaffa of the Claremont Institute has written a pamphlet called "Emancipating School Prayer." The subtitle is "How to Use the State Constitutions to Beat the ACLU and the Supreme Court."

Jaffa's idea is refreshingly simple. Forty-six of the 50 states have preambles invoking the name of God. Professor Jaffa proposes a joint resolution of Congress that declares "children in public schools might lawfully recite voluntary prayers employing only such acknowledgment of divine power and goodness as is present in their own state constitutions or in the constitutions of any of the other states."

"GRATEFUL TO ALMIGHTY GOD"

Here are excerpts from a few state constitutions that are quite representative of the others:

"We the people of the State of California, grateful to Almighty God for our freedom, in order to secure and perpetuate its blessings, do establish this Constitution."

"We the people of the State of Illinois—grateful to Almighty God for the civil, political and religious liberty which he has permitted us to enjoy and seeking his blessing upon our endeavors—do ordain and establish this Constitution for the State of Illinois."

"We the people of the State of Florida, being grateful to Almighty God for our constitutional liberty . . . do ordain and establish this constitution."

"We the people of Mississippi in convention assembled, grateful to Almighty God, and invoking his blessing on our work, do ordain and establish this constitution." The writers of the Mississippi Constitution, aware of legal mischievousness, added this provision in Article III, Section 18: "The rights hereby secured shall not be construed to . . . exclude the Holy Bible from use in any public school of this state."

Should this simple resolution be passed and signed by the president, I would join with Professor Jaffa in eager anticipation of the legal debate over whether the daily recitation by school children of that which is in their state's constitution is unconstitutional.

> "By using public funds for private, parochial schools, religious conservatives strike a blow against secular, public education."

TAX DOLLARS SHOULD NOT FUND RELIGIOUS SCHOOLS

Bob Peterson

Some public school districts have initiated a voucher system that allows children of low-income families to attend a private school of their choice, including religious schools. The voucher transfers the tax dollars that the public school would normally have received to the private school to pay at least part of the student's tuition. In the following viewpoint, Bob Peterson argues against the voucher system. Using public funds to support a religious school violates church-state separation, he contends. Furthermore, he asserts, the voucher system deprives public schools of funds that are desperately needed. Peterson, a fifth-grade teacher, was named 1995–1996 Wisconsin Elementary Teacher of the Year. He is also the editor of the education newspaper *Rethinking Schools*.

As you read, consider the following questions:
1. In Peterson's opinion, why are private schools not always better than public schools?
2. Who is behind the voucher movement, according to the author?
3. According to Peterson, how many times have referenda supporting voucher systems been defeated by state voters?

Reprinted from Bob Peterson, "Teacher of the Year Gives Vouchers a Failing Grade," *The Progressive*, April 1997, by permission of *The Progressive*, 409 E. Main St., Madison, WI 53703.

One recent winter morning, during the worst cold spell of the year, I found some caulk in my basement and took it to school. I teach at La Escuela Fratney in Milwaukee, Wisconsin, which was built in 1903. My classroom's third-floor windows are drafty, and on windy days, the kids who sit near the window often wear jackets to keep warm.

On this particular day, the wind chill was minus forty degrees. The big news—apart from the weather and the Superbowl—was that a Madison judge had declared the expansion of Milwaukee's school-voucher program unconstitutional.

I was relieved by the news. Republicans around the country have been pushing the idea of using publicly funded vouchers to send kids to private school. And Wisconsin has been in the forefront of this effort.

Vouchers are a top item on the conservative agenda. The religious right wants to use them to tear down the wall of separation between church and state. By using public funds for private, parochial schools, religious conservatives strike a blow against secular, public education. Vouchers serve that purpose, just as they serve the broader conservative movement's goal of cutting government entitlements and denying government responsibility for social services.

For sixteen years, I've taught public school in Milwaukee's central city, and I've been active in school reform. I know that vouchers won't seal the windows at La Escuela Fratney.

THE MILWAUKEE VOUCHER PROGRAM

Vouchers have been synonymous with Milwaukee ever since 1990, when Wisconsin began an experiment allowing low-income children in the city to use publicly funded vouchers to attend nonreligious private schools inside city boundaries. The courts upheld that original program. In the 1996–1997 school year, some 1,600 Milwaukee students received roughly $4,400 each to attend nonreligious private schools.

In 1995, the Wisconsin legislature expanded the Milwaukee voucher program to include religious schools and to allow as many as 15,000 students to take part, but the state suspended the expansion because of a lawsuit charging that it violates the state constitution. Until 1996, when Cleveland began a low-income voucher program that also included religious schools, Milwaukee had the only voucher experiment in the country. (Cleveland's program is also being challenged in the courts, but was allowed to proceed until a final ruling.)

One of the big myths of the school-choice movement is that

private schools are always better than public schools.
But in Milwaukee, vouchers gave rise to some fly-by-night private institutions.

The schools that initially took part in the voucher program were longstanding private institutions that, over the years, had built an infrastructure and a reputation attractive to tuition-paying students. Then the project started some new private schools—and they began to fail.

Two voucher schools closed unexpectedly in mid-year amid charges of inflated enrollment figures and missing or fraudulent financial records. Two others were unable to pay their staff regularly, leading to an exodus of teachers and students. A fifth school closed during the summer.

A VIOLATION OF CHURCH AND STATE

Religious schools normally charge less than nonsectarian private schools. Thus, a major consequence of a $3,000 voucher plan will be to direct tax-raised government money away from public schools and into church schools. This raises several constitutional questions.

If a major and foreseeable consequence of voucher plans is to funnel most of the money to church schools because the value of the voucher is set to coincide with what church schools charge, then this is precisely what the founders of this country sought to avoid: money raised from everyone's taxes used to support sectarian religious institutions.

Ira Glasser, *San Diego Union-Tribune*, September 27, 1996.

One of the schools that closed, the Milwaukee Preparatory School, may have been obliged to return up to $300,000 due to exaggerated enrollment figures, but the state could not complete an audit because of missing financial records. The school's founder skipped town. He was eventually arrested in Texas and charged with criminal fraud. Charges are still pending. The school had claimed in September 1995 that 175 out of its 200 students carried vouchers. By the time the school closed in February, only eighty students remained. Nine out of the twelve teachers had quit because the school hadn't paid them.

The director of another school, Exito Education Center, was charged with felony fraud for falsifying attendance records. During a John Doe proceeding, the school's former office manager told authorities that the director ordered her to fix the books, and threatened her wages if she did not comply. The director has twice failed to appear at court on the charges and a bench warrant has been issued.

In Milwaukee, the conservatives who clamor for higher standards and public-school accountability promoted a private voucher program with virtually no accountability measures. The private schools are not required to have a board of directors, adhere to open meetings or records laws, have grievance procedures for staff or students, or even administer state assessment tests.

It is harder to get a liquor license or set up a corner gas station in Milwaukee than it is to start a private school.

"To set up a school eligible for state funds under the school-choice program, almost all that a wannabe principal has to do is to hang out a shingle," the *Milwaukee Journal Sentinel* complained in an editorial last year. "Standards barely exist; oversight is minimal."

THE MUSCLE BEHIND THE VOUCHER MOVEMENT

The financial and legislative muscle behind vouchers comes from the conservative movement—national organizations such as the Heritage Foundation or the Institute for Justice; local think tanks such as the Wisconsin Policy Research Institute and the Heartland Institute; Republican politicians such as Wisconsin Governor Tommy Thompson and Ohio Governor George Voinovich. Conservative foundations have provided all-important funding.

Anyone looking into the voucher movement soon comes across two names: Michael Joyce of the Bradley Foundation and Clint Bolick of the Institute for Justice.

The Milwaukee-based Bradley Foundation, whose assets of $461 million make it the country's most powerful rightwing foundation, has poured millions of dollars into voucher initiatives. Bolick is a libertarian who is perhaps best known as the man who dubbed Lani Guinier "the quota queen."

The Bradley Foundation's president, Michael Joyce, has proclaimed vouchers the only educational reform worth pursuing. The foundation has awarded $5.8 million since 1992 to Partners Advancing Values in Education, a Milwaukee group that provides partial vouchers to students at religious schools. Bradley has also funneled almost $4.5 million to the Wisconsin Policy Research Institute, whose main education reform is vouchers. When Wisconsin Governor Tommy Thompson wanted to hire a "dream team" of private lawyers headed by Whitewater prosecutor Kenneth Starr to defend vouchers for religious schools, Bradley agreed to pony up $350,000 to the state so it could do so.

The Bradley Foundation also gave almost $1 million to Charles

Murray to research and co-author *The Bell Curve*. Among other things, the book argues that African Americans tend to be intellectually inferior to Asians and whites, and that educational resources should be targeted at the intellectual elite. Not surprisingly, the book's main educational reform is school choice, including public funds for religious schools.

Clint Bolick has been busy promoting vouchers in court cases around the country. He first did so while at the Landmark Legal Foundation (which between 1990 and 1992 received $310,000 from the Bradley Foundation), and then with the Institute for Justice. Bolick co-founded the Institute, which has received $425,000 in Bradley money. (He also helped launch the American Civil Rights Institute to dismantle affirmative-action programs.)

The conservative economist, Milton Friedman, came up with the idea of vouchers in the 1950s. Their first public use occurred in the South following the 1954 *Brown v. Board of Education* decision, when white people used vouchers to gain entrance to private academies to avoid attending public schools with African Americans. The courts ultimately struck down that use of vouchers.

During the 1996 Presidential primaries, the fractured Republican Party was of one mind on vouchers. Even Colin Powell, the man the social conservatives love to hate, supported publicly funded vouchers for private schools.

VOTER RESISTANCE TO VOUCHERS

Conservative politicians, who repeatedly cite the Milwaukee experiment, would love to put voucher programs on the national fast track. They have been hampered by legal questions and voter resistance—particularly in the suburbs. There, dissatisfaction with schools is low. And many suburbanites don't want inner-city students using vouchers to attend their schools. The four times that voucher referenda have been put before statewide voters, most recently in the state of Washington in 1996, they have failed by a 2-to-1 margin. (Colorado, California, and Oregon voters have also rejected statewide voucher schemes.)

Conservative voucher advocates love to highlight their support in the black community. Although it is not as popular as conservatives would like to believe, African American support of vouchers is not surprising. African Americans are poorly served by failing public schools and rightly disenchanted with public education.

But the conservative alliance with blacks is fragile.

In Milwaukee, the black politician most identified with

vouchers, Democratic state representative Annette "Polly" Williams, has increasingly distanced herself from the business and conservative community. She is particularly upset with attempts to allow private schools to screen students and with the business community's increasingly explicit goal of expanding vouchers to all students, not just low-income children.

"We have got our black agenda and they have got [their own] agenda," Williams has said of the business community. "I didn't see where their resources really were being used to empower us as much as to co-opt us."

EDUCATION AND DEMOCRACY

It is impossible to think about public education without understanding its relationship to democracy. There is no arena in this country with a comparable vision of equality—no matter how much this vision is tarnished in practice—and where people of different backgrounds interact on a daily basis.

When a Dane County, [Wisconsin] judge, Paul Higginbotham, decided against vouchers for religious schools, it was a blow to supporters of school choice around the country. Without the participation of religious schools, which account for about 85 percent of private-school students in Milwaukee, the voucher program can't expand much beyond the 1,600 students who now participate.

In his fifty-one-page ruling, Higginbotham concentrated on church-state issues. "Perhaps the most offensive part" of the voucher plan, he wrote, "is that it compels Wisconsin citizens of varying religious faiths to support schools with their tax dollars that proselytize students and attempt to inculcate them with beliefs contrary to their own. We do not object to the existence of parochial schools or that they attempt to spread their beliefs through their schools. They just cannot do it with state tax dollars."

Voucher supporters had argued that the expanded Milwaukee voucher program would not provide government support to religion but would merely help parents choose the best schools for their children. Higginbotham used promotional materials from those schools to dismiss that view. "The continuing purpose of St. Matthew Evangelical Lutheran Church and Schools is to go and tell the pure Gospel of Jesus Christ for the conversion of unbelievers and the strengthening of believers in faith and Christian living," reads one pamphlet.

As important as the church-state issues are, they are not the only concern.

EDUCATION'S REAL PROBLEMS

Vouchers are yet another diversion from the real problems in our failing urban schools. It's easy to chant the mantra of vouchers, as if they could magically transform education. It's much harder to do something about the real needs of urban public-school students.

As a classroom teacher, I am less concerned with competition from private schools than I am with my immediate problems: class size, inadequate facilities, and staff training.

Vouchers only aggravate the already troubling reality that our schools do not serve all children equally well. We have good schools, but they are clustered in affluent communities. There are huge differences between the schools in privileged suburbs and those in urban districts populated by low-income students and children of color.

Vouchers would take precious tax dollars from public schools and divert them to private schools. Milwaukee Superintendent Robert Jasna estimated that if the Milwaukee voucher program had been allowed to expand as planned by the legislature, the Milwaukee public schools could have lost as much as $100 million in funding over four years. They also make it possible for the Wisconsin legislature to pretend it is doing something about reforming the Milwaukee public schools while it ignores them.

Jonathan Kozol, author of *Savage Inequalities* and other books on education, said it best: "My own faith leads me to defend the genuinely ethical purposes of public education as a terrific American tradition, and to point to what it's done at its best— not simply for the very rich, but for the average American citizen. We need to place the voucher advocates, the enemies of public schools, where they belong: in the position of those who are subverting something decent in America."

| "Providing public funds for a child's education, whether or not that education is pursued in a religious setting, does no violence to the Constitution."

TAX DOLLARS SHOULD FUND RELIGIOUS SCHOOLS

Denis P. Doyle

Some low-income students are able to attend private schools through the use of vouchers, a payment system that transfers the tax dollars allotted for a student's education from the public school to the private school. In the following viewpoint, Denis P. Doyle defends this practice. Pointing out that more than half of the private schools in the United States are Catholic schools, he maintains that the policy of not supporting religious schools with taxpayer dollars was originally an expression of anti-Catholic sentiment. Doyle contends that to continue to exclude Catholic or other religious schools from government funding or voucher programs threatens the survival of some private, sectarian schools, which provide many valuable functions. Doyle is an education writer, analyst, and consultant.

As you read, consider the following questions:

1. According to Doyle, what racial group is more likely to prefer private schools?
2. The two kinds of public schools supported by the New England states until the mid–nineteenth century differed in what ways, according to the author?
3. What important function do Catholic schools fulfill, in Doyle's opinion?

Reprinted by permission of the author from "Vouchers for Religious Schools," by Denis P. Doyle, *The Public Interest*, no. 127 (Spring 1997), pp. 88–95; ©1997 by National Affairs, Inc.

The American public, if opinion polls are to be believed, overwhelmingly prefers private to public schools. A recent poll in *USA Today* reports that, among respondents with school-age children, 47 percent would use private schools "if they had the resources." Interest in private schools has a racial component as well; African Americans are much more likely to express a preference for private schools than whites, and, not surprisingly, African Americans report much lower levels of satisfaction with public schools than whites.

A FUNCTION OF FAMILY INCOME

The ability to attend private school, of course, is largely a function of family income. For, as the sociologist James Coleman once pointed out, private schools face a significant "tariff barrier"; not only must they charge tuition to generate income but their "competition"—public schools—are so heavily subsidized that they are "free" to consumers. At the same time, almost without exception, public policy forbids the use of public funds to attend private religious schools, which account for 85 percent of private-school enrollment. Yet, if private schools are good enough for the discerning and the well off, why are they not good enough for the poor and dispossessed?

It's no exaggeration to say that the last unserved minorities in America are poor children whose families prefer private religious schools to public schools. Such an educational opportunity is simply not available to the poor except through charity and private beneficence, the one activity the modern welfare state was designed to render unnecessary. Imagine denying Medicare recipients the right to seek medical care in a Jewish, Lutheran, or Catholic hospital because of its religious character, or forbidding a Social Security pensioner from using Social Security benefits to be buried in hallowed ground. Indeed, one wonders what the state interest is in denying children access to private religious schools. . . .

ANTI-CATHOLICISM AS PUBLIC POLICY

Few Americans are aware that the notion of "separation of church and state," insofar as it is used as a justification for excluding religious schools from public funding, is largely anti-Catholic in origin. Until the late 1840s, the states of New England supported two kinds of public schools, Protestant and what were euphemistically called "Irish schools." Both types of schools required students to engage in devotional activities—public prayer and Bible reading—but the Protestant schools used the King James version of the Bible while the Catholics used the Douay version. Not satisfied with the literary excellence of the Douay version, Protestant-dominated legislatures systematically began to disenfranchise "Irish schools." The nation was overcome by an unseemly nativism. Meanwhile, Protestant devotional activities—school prayer and Bible reading—continued without constitutional impediment until 1962, when they were struck down by the Court.

VOUCHING FOR A RELIGIOUS EDUCATION

Much of the debate [about whether students from low-income families can use school vouchers to attend religious schools] focus[es] on the serpentine wall between church and state.

When religious issues are ignored and vouchers are evaluated in educational terms, the findings are clear: Vouchers work for the inner-city poor. Low-income families receiving vouchers are pleased with their children's school, even when the grants amount to less than half what the public school spends. Voucher students are more apt to stay in school, learn more, and earn their high-school diploma. No wonder inner-city residents, when asked, strongly support school choice.

Paul E. Peterson, *Wall Street Journal*, December 5, 1995.

Indeed, so sure were the legislatures and courts that the practice of funding religious schools was legal—to either enfranchise or disenfranchise them as they saw fit—that no constitutional issues were thought to be involved. Not only was there no presumption of unconstitutionality, there was a positive presumption of constitutionality. It fell to James G. Blaine, a Republican from Maine, who served in the House of Representatives from 1863 to 1876 and was a colleague and friend of President Grant, to propose an amendment to the U.S. Constitution which would forever bar the "Popish" practice of providing aid to Catholic schools. Blaine and his supporters had no objection to religious education, so long as it was Protestant. Convinced of the necessity of protecting the young nation from foreign influences, the amendment—never enacted at the national level—was enacted, over time, in state after state, thus effectively eliminating aid to Catholic schools.

The overt anti-Catholicism of the Blaine amendment presents an extraordinary irony. Our first settlers were religious dissidents, and the United States was not hostile to religious differences at the time of the founding. To the contrary, the Northwest

Ordinance had made available gifts of land for religious schools, and the first schools in the original 13 colonies were denominational and enjoyed public funding. In fact, the architects of the modern public-school system, Horace Mann for example, were themselves deeply religious and saw the new "common school" as fulfilling religious—though interdenominational—functions. Robust Unitarian-Universalists, they were convinced that schools must provide moral uplift, which was best achieved, in their view, by ecumenical Protestantism.

In the modern era, of course, separation of church and state is offered as a principled reason for not aiding families who want to send their children to private school. Yet the roots of the practice are as poisonous as any civil right's affront of the modern era. Imagine framing a social policy in starkly anti-Catholic terms today. Indeed, the old saw springs to mind: Anti-Catholicism is the anti-Semitism of the liberal intellectual class. But, hostility to Catholics notwithstanding, the main "supplier" of private education in the United States is the Catholic church.

A CATHOLIC EDUCATION

Catholic schools make up more than one-half the private schools in the country, enrolling 53 percent of the nation's private-school students. The remaining attend either other types of religious schools (32 percent) or nonsectarian schools (15 percent). In the fall of 1990, there were 26,712 private elementary and secondary schools in the United States, enrolling 4.9 million students (contrasted to 89,000 public schools, enrolling 42 million students). To provide a sense of scale, about $25 billion of the total national expenditure of nearly $250 billion on elementary and secondary education is for private schools. A good rule of thumb is that private-school numbers represent about 10 percent of public-school numbers.

In 1930, Catholic schools enrolled 2.4 million youngsters out of a school-age population of approximately 26 million; in 1993, they enrolled 2.5 million youngsters out of a school-age population of 47 million youngsters. The high point of Catholic school enrollment was 1960, when 5.2 million students were enrolled (out of a school-age population of 36 million). Catholic schools were, during these early decades, among the most important socializing influences in America. They offered a safe haven for the immigrant and for immigrant families, providing a sense of familiarity and continuity in a confusing and often dangerous environment. Catholic schools acted as a buffer from the harsh realities of industrialization, a mediating structure that stood between the individual and the atomizing effects of unbridled free enterprise and anti-Catholic sentiment. Catholic schools, then, effectively fulfilled—and fulfill to this day—a public function, just as government schools do. They inculcate a sense of moral and civic duty in the student while providing the student with the necessary educational skills for further advancement.

Yet after World War II, as America began to suburbanize, Catholic school graduates moved from manual to white-collar work and found themselves free to move from the ghettoes. At the same time, the nation's Catholic Bishops decided not to underwrite the funding of a new network of Catholic schools outside the central cities where they had flourished for a century. Anti-Catholicism was slowly ebbing, and, as Catholics moved to the suburbs in large numbers, enrollments began to plummet.

At the same time, however, total private-school enrollment was climbing, from 10.7 percent in 1979 to 12.4 percent in 1985; which is to say, non-Catholic private-school enrollments were increasing. Part of the growth was found in non-denominational schools, but the vast majority was in old main-line denominations and among religious groups that had historically not been major players, e.g., Conservative and Orthodox Jews and Eastern Rite Christians such as Greek and Armenian Orthodox.

The most important effect of Catholic school decline, however, was to shrink the pool of low-cost private education for the poor. Indeed, until the late 1940s, Catholic schools were, by and large, supported from the collection plate. But increasing costs, a declining number of religious teachers, and higher salary demands from lay teachers meant that Catholic schools began to charge tuition. And it was the "deductibility" of tuition payments from federal income tax that sparked the first major lawsuits about church-state separation. While it was—and still is—constitutional to deduct voluntary contributions, the Court ruled that tuition payments were not deductible because they were not voluntary.

DON'T EXCLUDE RELIGIOUS SCHOOLS

Private schools should once again be made available to poor children. Yet the pressure to privatize, which is building across the nation, misses the most important part of the market: religiously affiliated schools. Chris Whittle, founder of the Edison Project, and John Golle, founder of Education Alternatives, argue that American public schools may be standing at the threshold of privatization, just as American health care was a decade ago. Indeed, the greatest hope of success for entrepreneurs like Whittle and Golle is the possibility of education vouchers, publicly funding parents rather than schools. They would not have to petition, hat-in-hand, school boards across the country. They would simply open their schools, a market would emerge, and private schools—public schools too—would sell their services to willing clients.

But, while it is presumptively constitutional for non-sectarian, private providers to participate in such a market, it is presumptively unconstitutional for religious schools to participate. An astonishing possibility emerges then: If voucher systems are created that do not include religious schools, religious schools may disappear.

Prosperous religious schools—Episcopal and Society of Friends schools, for example—and religious schools that exert as much cultural as religious pull—Armenian Orthodox or Orthodox Jewish schools, for example—as well as Christian fundamentalist schools, would not be much affected by being excluded from a voucher system. They would soldier on. The major impact would be to put other religiously affiliated schools at significant risk. Not only would they be competing with "free" public schools, they would be competing with "free" non-sectarian private schools.

As a nation, we labor under the ugly residual of more than a century of virulent anti-Catholicism, made all the worse by a steadfast refusal to acknowledge it. At issue is not ending "separation of church and state"—that is an old and honored tenet of the American constitutional and political tradition. Indeed, separating church and state is good for the church and good for the state—both are more vital for it. What is at issue, however, is the state's police power used to "separate church and child." Providing public funds for a child's education, whether or not that education is pursued in a religious setting, does no violence to the Constitution. And it is the last, best hope for many of the nation's poor children.

PERIODICAL BIBLIOGRAPHY

The following articles have been selected to supplement the diverse views presented in this chapter. Addresses are provided for periodicals not indexed in the *Readers' Guide to Periodical Literature*, the *Alternative Press Index*, the *Social Sciences Index*, or the *Index to Legal Periodicals and Books*.

Robert H. Bork — "What to Do About the First Amendment," *Commentary*, February 1995.

Joan Brown Campbell, James M. Dunn, and A. James Rudin — "Religious Liberty Requires Unceasing Vigilance," *USA Today*, September 1996.

Congressional Digest — "Prayer in Public Schools," January 1995.

Edd Doerr — "The School Choice Scam," *Humanist*, November/December 1997.

Ernest L. Fortin — "Pros and Cons of Disestablishment," *Crisis*, April 1995. Available from 1814½ N St. NW, Washington, DC 20036.

Rick Henderson — "Schools of Thought," *Reason*, January 1997.

Kathleen Horan — "Pray in School? Pray to Whom?" *New York Times*, September 9, 1995.

Richard Lacayo — "Parochial Politics," *Time*, September 23, 1996.

Barbara McEwan — "Public Schools, Religion, and Public Responsibility," *USA Today*, May 1997.

Steven T. McFarland — "The School Prayer Temptation," *Christianity Today*, January 9, 1995.

Robert H. Meneilly — "Government Is Not God's Work," *New York Times*, August 29, 1993.

Madalyn O'Hair — "The Matter of Prayer," *American Atheist*, August 1995.

Judd W. Patton — "The 'Wall of Separation' Between Church and State," *Freeman*, November 1995. Available from The Foundation for Economic Education, Irvington-on-Hudson, NY 10533.

Kevin Sack — "In South, Prayer Is a Form of Protest," *New York Times*, November 8, 1997.

CHAPTER 4

HOW DOES THE INTERNET AFFECT CIVIL LIBERTIES?

CHAPTER PREFACE

In 1997, more than 75 percent of all public libraries in the United States offered free Internet access to their patrons, with more going on-line every day. The Internet seems to be a perfect match for libraries; both provide information for their users on practically any subject. But the Internet's wide range of topics and opinions is putting public libraries in the middle of a free speech debate.

The public library is the sole source of Internet access for many Americans. Most parents do not want their children exposed to pornography and other offensive material that is easily accessible over the Internet. For this reason, some libraries have installed programs on their computers that filter or block objectionable material on-line. This action has raised charges of censorship by some librarians and commentators who believe that libraries should be committed to a free flow of ideas.

Critics charge that the filtering software programs block content that is protected by the First Amendment. Furthermore, opponents argue, because the programs cannot discriminate between obscene and informational material, much of the material blocked is inoffensive speech. They contend that barring access to objectionable websites is similar to cutting out offensive articles from an encyclopedia.

Supporters of the filter programs maintain that the blocking of an occasional worthwhile website is an acceptable price to pay to maintain the community's traditional values and to protect children from exposure to sexually explicit material. Moreover, they assert, rather than being a tool for censorship, the software that prevents patrons from viewing obscene material is the equivalent of a librarian's decision not to add a particular book or magazine to the library's collection. Supporters explain that libraries are not required by the First Amendment to fulfill all requests for material; therefore, filtering websites does not fall under the definition of censorship

The advancing technology of the Internet has had an effect not only on free speech but on the right to privacy as well. The authors in the following chapter debate how the Internet has affected these civil liberty issues.

"The rapid growth of huge computer networks . . . raise[s] concerns about whether confidential information can be kept that way."

THE INTERNET THREATENS THE RIGHT TO PRIVACY

Nathaniel Sheppard Jr.

In the following viewpoint, Nathaniel Sheppard Jr. argues that the Internet threatens an individual's right to privacy. It is easy for Internet website owners and computer hackers to glean personal data by following the trails left behind by Web surfers, he asserts. Sheppard contends that the right to privacy is also threatened by businesses and governments that store personal information on computers, which are vulnerable to computer hackers. Sheppard is a contributing columnist to *Emerge* magazine.

As you read, consider the following questions:

1. What do "sniffer" programs do, according to Sheppard?
2. Why was Kevin Mitnick on the FBI's list of most-wanted hackers, according to the author?
3. How can computer users protect their privacy, in Sheppard's opinion?

Reprinted from Nathaniel Sheppard Jr., "Information Access Muddies Privacy Rights," *Emerge*, January 1997, by permission of the author.

Having promoted the Internet as one of the most important developments since sliced bread, let me now deal with an important shortcoming: potentially serious gaps in user privacy.

E-mail, for example, travels over the Net fast and furiously, but because it is relayed via numerous transfer points it is subject to interception by cunning hackers or unintended distribution by malfunctioning mail servers. During a trial period with a New York–based Internet service, I received more than 30 pieces of e-mail intended for others, some of it fairly provocative. I declined that service.

SENSITIVE INFORMATION

Credit card numbers and passwords also are vulnerable, as is sensitive information from medical records that insurers could use to deny coverage and that detractors could use to humiliate or manipulate.

Hackers sometimes use "sniffer" programs that cruise the Net looking for the first string of characters transmitted during log-on or after connection to commercial services. These electronic fishing trips sometimes capture screen names, passwords or credit card information.

And when you cruise the World Wide Web, you leave an electronic trail that computer-savvy individuals and companies can follow to see which sites you visited, how long you were there and what documents or photographs you viewed. That is how you get that junk e-mail.

In April 1996, Kevin Mitnick pleaded guilty to federal charges of using stolen mobile phone numbers. But the plea, in a North Carolina federal court stemming from a San Francisco Bay–area case, did not tell the whole story. He had earned the dubious distinction of being one of the FBI's most-wanted hackers because of a series of Internet break-ins.

Among other things, Mitnick was accused of using the Internet to gain access to corporate trade secrets and to capture more than 20,000 credit card numbers.

Perhaps even more alarming are the legal efforts by corporations and other businesses to gain access to a wide variety of personal data from municipalities on issues such as arrest records and financial and health records, with the intent of selling the information to anyone with a computer and high-speed modem.

At risk is sensitive data such as who has AIDS or a genetic disposition toward life-threatening diseases such as hypertension or sickle cell anemia; who is affected by alcohol or drug abuse, and who may have tried to commit suicide or displayed other indications of mental instability.

Maryland authorities have created a statewide mega-database of medical records that would contain detailed patient histories, a move some members of the Maryland Psychiatric Society call frightening and Big Brotherish.

Privacy Is Under Attack

In Illinois, the communications giant Ameritech Corp. was close to clinching a deal in Cook County, which includes Chicago, that would have given it exclusive electronic rights to sell all criminal and civil court records, except those in probate, that are currently electronically filed via modem.

The information would have become part of Ameritech's CivicLink, an on-line system that first was set up in Indianapolis in 1994. It is the rapid growth of huge computer networks such as this and the growing sophistication of hackers that raise concerns about whether confidential information can be kept that way. "There are privacy issues that must be considered here," says Donald O'Connell, chief judge of the Circuit Court of Cook County, who blocked the Ameritech deal.

"UH-OH!... I THINK I JUST DELETED OUR PRIVACY!"

Bob Gorrell for the Richmond Times-Dispatch. Reprinted with permission.

"The bad news is your privacy is under attack from many directions," says Andre Bacard, author of the Computer Privacy Handbook (Peachpit Press). "Do you know that Big Brother, and I, for that matter, can easily search and monitor all of your personal, sexual and political Usenet postings? Do you know that your e-mail, medical, financial and telephone records could be available to criminals, snoops and/or Big Brother for a cheap price?"

HOW TO PROTECT ON-LINE PRIVACY

Computer users can breathe a little easier, however, because of software programs and on-line services that are emerging to plug some of the security gaps. Among these are Pretty Good Privacy, an encryption program and www.anonymizer.com, a Web site that allows you to surf the Net without a trail. Other programs offer a variety of ways of protecting passwords and credit card information sent over the Net.

And in Congress, a bipartisan effort is underway to come up with legislation to regulate medical data banks. But a comprehensive solution remains far away.

In the meantime, watch out for traps as you cruise the info superhighway. Computer users should never write anything in e-mail that they would not want to see in print later; never send credit card information or other sensitive data over unsecured lines, and consider paying cash for medical services where possible, rather than using insurance, as a way of keeping files private.

> "Of course, the [website] owner knows what you're doing while you're there. What place, other than your own home, can you go where it will allow you full anonymity?"

THE INTERNET'S INVASION OF PRIVACY IS EXAGGERATED

Joseph Burns

In the following viewpoint, Joseph Burns argues that the concern about the invasion of personal privacy by the owners of websites on the Internet has been blown out of proportion. He asserts that all businesses—on the Internet or not—keep track of who their customers are. Furthermore, he maintains, no business knows any personal information about their customers unless it is given to them, which is not an invasion of privacy. What consumers should truly be concerned about, he contends, is the selling of their personal data by businesses without permission. Burns is an assistant professor of communications specializing in Internet issues at Susquehanna University in Selinsgrove, Pennsylvania.

As you read, consider the following questions:

1. According to Burns, why must website owners know who is using their sites?
2. What does a cookie do, according to the author?
3. In the author's opinion, what should happen to website owners who give out their customers' personal information without permission?

Reprinted from Joseph Burns, "Perfidious Peepers Trolling the Internet?" *The Washington Times*, July 5, 1997, by permission of *The Washington Times*.

C an the Internet do no right? First it was going to cocoon us all in our houses, then it was going to replace dating, then it was corrupting the youth by showing dirty pictures. Now the Internet, particularly the World Wide Web (WWW), is delving into our privacy.

PRIVACY ISSUES

The new anti-WWW buzzwords are "privacy issues."

The Federal Trade Commission is holding sessions on the subject. PC Magazine's Yael Li-Ron writes that there is a "great deal of risk" in going on-line. Survey results released in early June 1997 suggest that going on-line sets up a "personal intrusion" and CNN's Greg Lefevre writes that personal information is "scooped up" when you use the World Wide Web.

It is? Really?

So what does the WWW do that has people so nervous? One concern that is always brought up is that the owners of WWW sites know when your computer is in their site, and they know what is being done while you're there. And? Of course an owner knows a computer is using their site and the local K mart knows when you're in their store.

When you use the WWW, you make a request of the system to show text and image files. If the machine didn't know you were there, how would it know to whom to give the files?

Of course, the owner knows what you're doing while you're there. What place, other than your own home, can you go where it will allow you full anonymity and free reign over all inside? At least you're not being videotaped sitting at your computer. K mart does that.

Another concern is that the owner knows how long you've been in the site. Have you looked at your phone bill lately? The number and city are displayed down to the second. Are we upset at them also?

Ask someone whether they would enter their credit-card number over the Internet. I'll bet you'll receive a strong reaction against the idea, even though extensive measures have been taken to set up number encryption systems. Yet people will happily give their credit-card numbers over the phone to a stranger in a mail-order transaction or hand their card to a waiter who then goes to a separate room to write up the sale.

Read through most any story on Internet privacy and the "cookie" will be thrown around as the ultimate evil. A "cookie" is the nickname given to the little text files that some servers place on your computer when you enter their site. The file acts as a tag on your computer. The cookie allows the site to track how many times your computer comes to the site. The WWW site still has no idea who "you" are.

COOKIES ARE HARMLESS

Cookies . . . are the little data files that can be placed on your computer's hard drive by Web sites you visit. Web site hosts use them to speed your visit and to collect information about how you surf.

Because of the apparent invasiveness of this technique . . . the practice alarms some people. . . .

But the fears are overblown. . . .

Cookies don't prowl through your e-mail, extract your credit record or steal your passwords.

Mike Francis, *San Diego Union-Tribune ComputerLink*, February 24, 1998.

This may sound sinister, but in reality the use of a cookie is far more to track macro-level traffic than one specific person. Have you noticed all the advertising banners on WWW pages lately? Those advertisers would like some statistics on how many people come into the site and how long they stay. And the WWW site still has no idea who "you" are.

I often hear discussion that WWW sites use these cookies to gather your name and address. That's not completely true. In fact, the articles I've read on the subject do mention that cookies can contain names if the user "gives up his or her name." That doesn't sound like invasion to me. Without cooperation, you're just a computer stopping by to grab another file.

Now we get into the correct argument: What sites are doing with the names they are given, and the lack of adequate disclosure that cookies are being distributed. Those are true concerns. WWW site owners who give out names and personal data collected on site without getting permission or notifying the user upon their entry should be prosecuted and shut down.

Most people do not have a clear understanding of what the WWW is, or how it works. The system doesn't have the ability to gather your personal history when you look at a home page. So the media should not imply such a thing, when discussing privacy issues.

I wonder if those who proclaim loudest that the Internet should be totally anonymous are upset because of a true love of privacy for all or because they are going into sites they'd really rather others didn't know about?

| "Children must be protected from on-line predators, and they must be protected from Internet pornography."

INDECENT MATERIAL ON THE INTERNET SHOULD BE CENSORED

Shyla Welch

Numerous studies have concluded that exposure to pornography negatively affects the attitudes and behaviors of adults. In the following viewpoint, Shyla Welch argues that allowing children to be exposed to pornography over the Internet threatens society's future. She maintains that the U.S. Supreme Court has ruled that regulating some types of speech, such as obscene speech, does not violate the First Amendment. Therefore, Welch contends, indecent material on the Internet should be regulated to protect the best interests of children and society. Welch is the communications officer of Enough Is Enough!, an antipornography organization based in Fairfax, Virginia.

As you read, consider the following questions:

1. According to the author, why does no quantitative research exist showing how pornography affects children?
2. Why are children particularly vulnerable to exploitation on the Internet, in Welch's opinion?
3. What are the three communities that must work together to protect children on-line, according to Welch?

From Shyla Welch, "Should the Internet Be Regulated? Some Control Is Needed." This article appeared in the February 1998 issue and is reprinted with permission from *The World & I*, a publication of The Washington Times Corporation, ©1998.

A great deal of controversy surrounds the issue of regulating the Internet, particularly the possible regulation of Internet pornography. Opponents of such regulation sound the alarm: "Today pornography, tomorrow religion and politics."

This seeming inability to discern the difference between pornography and religion, politics, or other components of American life is, frankly, baffling. The difference can be understood by examining the nature of pornography and its negative impact on society.

THE NATURE OF PORNOGRAPHY

Pornography provides a one-dimensional portrayal of women. In pornography, women are insatiable sex machines, completely indiscriminate in their tastes and behaviors. In pornography, women want to be raped, because no means yes. In pornography, women want to wear dog collars and be tied with leather straps. In pornography, women want to be forced to have sex with animals, be urinated upon, be pierced and tortured and beaten to the edge of death.

Even the mildest pornography, in vast minority on the Internet, poses women so they are vulnerable and eager to please the unseen viewing male.

Because such depictions rarely satisfy the viewer for long, pornography increases in its rawness until no question can exist that the woman portrayed has lost a portion of her humanity and certainly her dignity.

Such objectification of women shapes the viewer's attitudes, with a particularly significant impact on youngsters still forming their attitudes about sexuality. The ease of access to on-line pornography, both intentionally by curious youngsters and unintentionally by children using the word search "toys" and receiving links to "Adult Sex Toys," bespeaks the need to afford young people a measure of protection in cyberspace.

Quantitative research showing how pornography affects children does not exist because such research would be unethical, but quantitative research showing the many harms of pornography to adults exists in abundance. Logical consistency dictates that if pornography affects the attitudes and behaviors of adults, it most certainly does so with vulnerable children. Furthermore, qualitative research showing pornography's effects on children does exist, and evidence certainly exists—evidence based on criminal reports and victims' stories.

Exposure of children to pornography is not problematic merely because they may see something they are too young to recognize as deviant behavior, although research indicating that images leave an unerasable imprint on the brain certainly causes concern.

Nor is the problem that children receive one antisocial message to counteract an abundance of prosocial messages; the problem is that the messages sent to children are increasingly antisocial. Asking children to ignore this bombardment of messages is asking them to do something a majority of adults cannot do themselves.

To suggest that children, who form their beliefs about the world through observation, must be allowed access to this portrayal of women and sexuality because adult access to this material must not be slowed by a nanosecond lest we lose our freedoms, is to place the culture's future on the hope that children will somehow not be influenced or damaged by the images presented them. Such hope is futile in light of the mountains of data proving that images influence attitudes and behaviors in adults, and certainly in children.

The Internet is particularly fascinating to children because they have access to an entire world through a computer and a modem. Cyberspace, however, is not some unique world functioning independently of the tangible world but is rather a reflection of the world inhabited by human beings. Like the real world, cyberspace consists of good and bad information, of well-intentioned individuals and individuals who take advantage of relative anonymity to exploit and harm. Children are particularly vulnerable to exploitation because of their innate curiosity and limited ability to recognize that situations are not necessarily as they appear.

CHILDREN NEED PROTECTION

The difference in how things appear and how they actually are has helped make the Internet a pedophile's playground. Even the most savvy of children are relatively trusting, and strangers pretending to be peers or offering "interesting" pictures find children easy prey on the Internet. Children must be protected from on-line predators, and they must be protected from Internet pornography.

Certainly, parents have the lion's share of responsibility in protecting their children. At no time in our society's history, however, have we expected parents to bear such a burden alone.

Traditionally, parents trying to teach their children to be responsible, productive members of society had the support of that society; certainly, society did not work at cross purposes with them under the guise of preserving "freedom." A recognition existed that society has a stake in the character development of its members and that shielding children from harm was in the best interest of civilized society.

NEWS ITEM: COURT UPHOLDS CYBERSPACE PORN!

Ed Gamble for the *Florida Times-Union*. Reprinted with permission.

As a society, we protect children from tobacco and alcohol until they reach an age where we deem they can make appropriate decisions. Through our laws, we seem to recognize that the ability to make decisions matures with age and experience. And we do not seem particularly terrified that the regulation of tobacco and alcohol sales will reduce the level of "adult" pleasures to a level appropriate for six-year-olds, an argument commonly posed when any suggestion is made of protecting children on-line.

Other arguments remind us that we already have child pornography and obscenity laws in cyberspace. Since most Americans may not understand the nuances of pornography laws, however, they may not realize that adult pornography such as *Playboy* and *Penthouse*, which is illegal for children in print and broadcast media, may be legally distributed to children in cyberspace.

Even worse, because there is no law against providing children indecency in cyberspace, and because obscenity is considered "indecency" until it has received due process, anyone providing children with violent, deviant pornography may do so without fear of legal recourse.

NOT ALL SPEECH IS PROTECTED SPEECH

The argument against any kind of regulation of cyberspace is frequently peppered with references to the First Amendment and "censorship," ignoring the fact that the Supreme Court has consistently ruled that not all speech is protected speech. Laws prohibiting false advertising, libel, slander, and speech threatening the safety of others (i.e., yelling "fire" in a crowded theater) have long been accepted as regulations a civilized society may place on conduct. Are we now, as a society, considering allowing the Internet to be a haven for those wanting to wreak their antisocial behavior on the rest of the world? What special qualities does the Internet possess to afford freedom from accountability to those who seek to harm and exploit children?

A THREE-PRONGED PARTNERSHIP

Every member of society has a stake in the future of the culture. Individuals must behave responsibly, with parents monitoring their children's computer use and taking every possible precaution to protect their children on-line. The technology community must also behave responsibly, by providing parents with sophisticated tools to help protect children, segregating adult pornography away from children, and removing illegal pornography from its proprietary boards and services. These two communities constitute two prongs of what should be a three-pronged partnership.

We must recognize that even if the vast majority of individuals and organizations are behaving responsibly, there will always be those who exploit others, particularly vulnerable children. The third prong of the partnership is the legal community; it must enforce laws already in place and ensure that laws are enacted to hold individuals who would use the Internet to harm others as responsible for their behavior in cyberspace as they would be in the real world.

The Internet has a great deal of information and entertainment to offer, but it should not be a refuge for behavior deemed unacceptable in society. Citizens with a government of, by, and for the people are reasonable to expect laws regarding conduct in cyberspace that are consistent with laws in the real world. If "free speech" in cyberspace means license to do anything to anyone, then such license in the real world cannot be far behind. At the end of that road, God help us all.

"The Internet is entitled to the same broad free speech protections given to books, magazines, and casual conversation."

CENSORING INDECENT MATERIAL ON THE INTERNET VIOLATES FREE SPEECH

American Civil Liberties Union

The American Civil Liberties Union (ACLU) is an organization dedicated to protecting the rights guaranteed by the U.S. Constitution. In the following viewpoint, the ACLU argues that free speech is threatened by software programs that would rate or block controversial material on the Internet. These programs will censor objectionable speech by making it invisible on the Internet, the organization contends. The ACLU asserts that if these programs are allowed to filter content, the Internet's diversity will be jeopardized and it could become a bland and homogenized medium.

As you read, consider the following questions:

1. How has a scenario to establish censorship on the Internet already been set in motion, according to the ACLU?
2. How does the ACLU illustrate its opinion that requiring citizens to self-rate their speech on the Internet offends the First Amendment?
3. What are some of the problems with user-based blocking software programs, according to the author?

Excerpted from the American Civil Liberties Union white paper "Fahrenheit 451.2: Is Cyberspace Burning? How Rating and Blocking Proposals May Torch Free Speech on the Internet," 1997. Reprinted by permission of the American Civil Liberties Union.

Any content-based regulation of the Internet, no matter how benign the purpose, could burn the global village to roast the pig.

—U.S. Supreme Court majority decision,
Reno v. ACLU (June 26, 1997)

In his chilling (and prescient) novel about censorship, *Fahrenheit 451*, author Ray Bradbury describes a futuristic society where books are outlawed. "Fahrenheit 451" is, of course, the temperature at which books burn.

In Bradbury's novel—and in the physical world—people censor the printed word by burning books. But in the virtual world, one can just as easily censor controversial speech by banishing it to the farthest corners of cyberspace using rating and blocking programs. Today, will Fahrenheit, version 451.2—a new kind of virtual censorship—be the temperature at which cyberspace goes up in smoke?

The first flames of Internet censorship appeared in 1995, with the introduction of the Federal Communications Decency Act (CDA), outlawing "indecent" online speech. But in the landmark case *Reno v. ACLU*, the Supreme Court overturned the CDA, declaring that the Internet is entitled to the highest level of free speech protection. In other words, the Court said that online speech deserved the protection afforded to books and other printed matter.

Today, all that we have achieved may now be lost, if not in the bright flames of censorship then in the dense smoke of the many ratings and blocking schemes promoted by some of the very people who fought for freedom. And in the end, we may find that the censors have indeed succeeded in "burning down the house to roast the pig."

Is Cyberspace Burning?

The ashes of the CDA were barely smoldering when the White House called a summit meeting to encourage Internet users to self-rate their speech and to urge industry leaders to develop and deploy the tools for blocking "inappropriate" speech. The meeting was "voluntary," of course: the White House claimed it wasn't holding anyone's feet to the fire.

The American Civil Liberties Union (ACLU) and others in the cyber-liberties community were genuinely alarmed by the tenor of the White House summit and the unabashed enthusiasm for technological fixes that will make it easier to block or render invisible controversial speech.

Industry leaders responded to the White House call with a

barrage of announcements:

- Netscape announced plans to join Microsoft—together the two giants have 90% or more of the web browser market—in adopting PICS (Platform for Internet Content Selection), the rating standard that establishes a consistent way to rate and block online content;
- IBM announced it was making a $100,000 grant to RSAC (Recreational Software Advisory Council) to encourage the use of its RSACi rating system. Microsoft Explorer already employs the RSACi ratings system, Compuserve encourages its use and it is fast becoming the de facto industry standard rating system;
- Four of the major search engines—the services which allow users to conduct searches of the Internet for relevant sites—announced a plan to cooperate in the promotion of "self-regulation" of the Internet. The president of one, Lycos, was quoted in a news account as having "thrown down the gauntlet" to the other three, challenging them to agree to exclude unrated sites from search results;
- Following the announcement of proposed legislation by Sen. Patty Murray (D-Wash.), which would impose civil and ultimately criminal penalties on those who mis-rate a site, the makers of the blocking program Safe Surf proposed similar legislation, the "Online Cooperative Publishing Act."

But it was not any one proposal or announcement that caused our alarm; rather, it was the failure to examine the longer-term implications for the Internet of rating and blocking schemes.

A Bland and Homogenized Internet

What may be the result? The Internet will become bland and homogenized. The major commercial sites will still be readily available; they will have the resources and inclination to self-rate, and third-party rating services will be inclined to give them acceptable ratings. People who disseminate quirky and idiosyncratic speech, create individual home pages, or post to controversial news groups, will be among the first Internet users blocked by filters and made invisible by the search engines. Controversial speech will still exist, but will only be visible to those with the tools and know-how to penetrate the dense smokescreen of industry "self-regulation."

As bad as this very real prospect is, it can get worse. Faced with the reality that, although harder to reach, sex, hate speech and other controversial matter is still available on the Internet, how long will it be before governments begin to make use of an Internet already configured to accommodate massive censorship? If you look at these various proposals in a larger context, a very plausible scenario emerges. It is a scenario which in some respects has already been set in motion:

- First, the use of PICS becomes universal; providing a uniform method for content rating.
- Next, one or two rating systems dominate the market and become the de facto standard for the Internet.
- PICS and the dominant rating system(s) are built into Internet software as an automatic default.
- Unrated speech on the Internet is effectively blocked by these defaults.
- Search engines refuse to report on the existence of unrated or "unacceptably" rated sites.
- Governments frustrated by "indecency" still on the Internet make self-rating mandatory and mis-rating a crime.

The scenario is, for now, theoretical—but inevitable. It is clear that any scheme that allows access to unrated speech will fall afoul of the government-coerced push for a "family friendly" Internet. We are moving inexorably toward a system that blocks speech simply because it is unrated and makes criminals of those who mis-rate.

The White House meeting was clearly the first step in that direction and away from the principle that protection of the electronic word is analogous to protection of the printed word. Despite the Supreme Court's strong rejection of a broadcast analogy for the Internet, government and industry leaders alike are now inching toward the dangerous and incorrect position that the Internet is like television, and should be rated and censored accordingly.

Is Cyberspace burning? Not yet, perhaps. But where there's smoke, there's fire.

FREE SPEECH ONLINE: A VICTORY UNDER SIEGE

On June 26, 1997, the Supreme Court held in *Reno v. ACLU* that the Communications Decency Act, which would have made it a crime to communicate anything "indecent" on the Internet, violated the First Amendment. It was the nature of the Internet itself, and the quality of speech on the Internet, that led the Court to declare that the Internet is entitled to the same broad free speech protections given to books, magazines, and casual conversation.

The ACLU argued, and the Supreme Court agreed, that the CDA was unconstitutional because, although aimed at protecting minors, it effectively banned speech among adults. Similarly, many of the rating and blocking proposals, though designed to limit minors' access, will inevitably restrict the ability of adults to communicate on the Internet. In addition, such proposals will restrict the rights of older minors to gain access to material that clearly has value for them.

RETHINKING THE RUSH TO RATE

This viewpoint examines the free speech implications of the various proposals for Internet blocking and rating. Individually, each of the proposals poses some threat to open and robust speech on the Internet; some pose a considerably greater threat than others.

Even more ominous is the fact that the various schemes for rating and blocking, taken together, could create a black cloud of private "voluntary" censorship that is every bit as threatening as the CDA itself to what the Supreme Court called "the most participatory form of mass speech yet developed."

We call on industry leaders, Internet users, policy makers and parents groups to engage in a genuine debate about the free speech ramifications of the rating and blocking schemes being proposed. . . .

SELF-RATING SCHEMES ARE WRONG FOR THE INTERNET

To begin with, the notion that citizens should "self-rate" their speech is contrary to the entire history of free speech in America. A proposal that we rate our online speech is no less offensive to the First Amendment than a proposal that publishers of books and magazines rate each and every article or story, or a proposal that everyone engaged in a street corner conversation rate his or her comments. But that is exactly what will happen to books, magazines, and any kind of speech that appears online under a self-rating scheme.

In order to illustrate the very practical consequences of these schemes, consider [one reason] why the ACLU is against self-rating:

CONTROVERSIAL SPEECH WILL BE CENSORED

Kiyoshi Kuromiya, founder and sole operator of Critical Path Aids Project, has a web site that includes safer sex information written in street language with explicit diagrams, in order to reach the widest possible audience. Kuromiya doesn't want to apply the rating "crude" or "explicit" to his speech, but if he doesn't, his site will be blocked as an unrated site. If he does rate, his speech will be lumped in with "pornography" and blocked from view. Under either choice, Kuromiya has been effectively blocked from reaching a large portion of his intended audience—teenage Internet users—as well as adults.

As this example shows, the consequences of rating are far from neutral. The ratings themselves are all pejorative by definition, and they result in certain speech being blocked. . . .

IS THIRD-PARTY RATING THE ANSWER?

Third-party ratings systems, designed to work in tandem with PICS labeling, have been held out by some as the answer to the free speech problems posed by self-rating schemes. On the plus side, some argue, ratings by an independent third party could minimize the burden of self-rating on speakers and could reduce the inaccuracy and mis-rating problems of self-rating. In fact, one of the touted strengths of the original PICS proposal was that a variety of third-party ratings systems would develop and users could pick and choose from the system that best fit their values. But third-party ratings systems still pose serious free speech concerns.

First, a multiplicity of ratings systems has not yet emerged on the market, probably due to the difficulty of any one company or organization trying to rate over a million web sites, with hundreds of new sites—not to mention discussion groups and chat rooms—springing up daily.

UNRATED SITES MAY BE BLOCKED

Second, under third-party rating systems, unrated sites still may be blocked.

When choosing which sites to rate first, it is likely that third-party raters will rate the most popular web sites first, marginalizing individual and non-commercial sites. And like the self-rating systems, third-party ratings will apply subjective and value-laden ratings that could result in valuable material being blocked to adults and older minors. In addition, available third-party rating systems have no notification procedure, so speakers have no way of knowing whether their speech has received a negative rating.

The fewer the third-party ratings products available, the greater the potential for arbitrary censorship. Powerful industry forces may lead one product to dominate the marketplace. If, for example, virtually all households use Microsoft Internet Explorer and Netscape, and the browsers, in turn, use RSACi as their system, RSACi could become the default censorship system for the Internet. In addition, federal and state governments could pass laws mandating use of a particular ratings system in schools or libraries. Either of these scenarios could devastate the diversity of the Internet marketplace.

Pro-censorship groups have argued that a third-party rating system for the Internet is no different from the voluntary Motion Picture Association of America ratings for movies that we've all lived with for years. But there is an important distinction: only a finite number of movies are produced in a given year. In contrast, the amount of content on the Internet is infinite. Movies are a static, definable product created by a small number of producers; speech on the Internet is seamless, interactive, and conversational. MPAA ratings also don't come with automatic blocking mechanisms.

THE PROBLEMS WITH USER-BASED BLOCKING SOFTWARE

With the explosive growth of the Internet, and in the wake of the recent censorship battles, the marketplace has responded with a wide variety of user-based blocking programs. Each company touts the speed and efficiency of its staff members in blocking speech that they have determined is inappropriate for minors. The programs also often block speech based on keywords. (This can result in sites such as www.middlesex.gov or www.SuperBowlXXX.com being blocked because they contain the keywords "sex" and "XXX.")

In *Reno v. ACLU*, the ACLU successfully argued that the CDA violated the First Amendment because it was not the least restrictive means of addressing the government's asserted interest in protecting children from inappropriate material. In supporting this argument, we suggested that a less restrictive alternative was the availability of user-based blocking programs, e.g. Net Nanny, that parents could use in the home if they wished to limit their child's Internet access.

While user-based blocking programs present troubling free speech concerns, we still believe today that they are far preferable to any statute that imposes criminal penalties on online speech. In contrast, many of the new ratings schemes pose far greater free speech concerns than do user-based software programs.

Each user installs the program on her home computer and turns the blocking mechanism on or off at will. The programs do not generally block sites that they haven't rated, which means that they are not 100 percent effective. Unlike the third-party ratings or self-rating schemes, these products usually do not work in concert with browsers and search engines, so the home user rather than an outside company sets the defaults. (However, it should be noted that this "stand alone" feature could theoretically work against free speech principles, since here, too, it would be relatively easy to draft a law mandating the use of the products, under threat of criminal penalties.)

PARENTAL SUPERVISION IS REQUIRED

Existing laws already make it illegal to distribute obscene material in any form to minors. Those laws should be strictly enforced. There are also other ways to protect children on-line that do not curtail anyone's freedom of information or free speech, the best and most important being parental supervision. As with reading or TV viewing, children benefit most when they have the time and attention of parents who teach them to make good choices.

Virginia McCurley, *Christian Science Monitor*, March 27, 1997.

While the use of these products avoids some of the larger control issues with ratings systems, the blocking programs are far from problem-free. A number of products have been shown to block access to a wide variety of information that many would consider appropriate for minors. For example, some block access to safer sex information, although the Supreme Court has held that teenagers have the right to obtain access to such information even without their parent's consent. Other products block access to information of interest to the gay and lesbian community. Some products even block speech simply because it criticizes their product.

Some products allow home users to add or subtract particular sites from a list of blocked sites. For example, a parent can decide to allow access to "playboy.com" by removing it from the blocked sites list, and can deny access to "powerrangers.com" by adding it to the list. However most products consider their lists of blocked speech to be proprietary information which they will not disclose. . . .

PRELIMINARY INFORMATION ON THE NET

In fact, many speakers on the Net provide preliminary information about the nature of their speech. The ACLU's site on America Online, for example, has a message on its home page announcing that the site is a "free speech zone." Many sites offering commercial transactions on the Net contain warnings concerning the security of Net information. Sites containing sexually explicit material often begin with a statement describing the adult nature of the material. Chat rooms and newsgroups have names that describe the subject being discussed. Even individual e-mail messages contain a subject line.

The preliminary information available on the Internet has several important components that distinguish it from all the ratings systems discussed above: (1) It is created and provided by the speaker; (2) It helps the user decide whether to read any further; (3) Speakers who choose not to provide such information are not penalized; (4) It does not result in the automatic blocking of speech by an entity other than the speaker or reader before the speech has ever been viewed. Thus, the very nature of the Internet reveals why more speech is always a better solution than censorship for dealing with speech that someone may find objectionable.

It is not too late for the Internet community to slowly and carefully examine these proposals and to reject those that will transform the Internet from a true marketplace of ideas into just another mainstream, lifeless medium with content no more exciting or diverse than that of television.

Civil libertarians, human rights organizations, librarians and Internet users, speakers and providers all joined together to defeat the CDA. We achieved a stunning victory, establishing a legal framework that affords the Internet the highest constitutional protection. We put a quick end to a fire that was all but visible and threatening. The fire next time may be more difficult to detect—and extinguish.

5

"Our Founding Fathers recognized that an absolute right to privacy was incompatible with an ordered society."

COMPUTER ENCRYPTION THREATENS PUBLIC SAFETY

Robert S. Litt

Robert S. Litt is the deputy assistant attorney general for the Criminal Division of the Department of Justice. In the following viewpoint, Litt contends that allowing the computer industry to develop unbreakable encryption to protect the privacy of their computer files is a grave threat to public safety. While law enforcement agencies welcome strong encryption, Litt maintains, the public's right to privacy must be balanced against the needs of national security. Therefore, he argues, law enforcement must be given the keys to all computer encryption codes to protect the public from terrorism and other threats.

As you read, consider the following questions:

1. What examples does Litt give to support his contention that unbreakable encryption codes could cripple law enforcement efforts?
2. According to Litt, how long would it take a supercomputer to decrypt a single message using 56-bit DES?
3. In the author's opinion, how do export controls on strong encryption products serve an important role in law enforcement?

Reprinted from Robert S. Litt's testimony in *Security and Freedom Through Encryption (SAFE) Act*, a hearing before the Subcommittee on Courts and Intellectual Property of the Committee on the Judiciary of the House of Representatives, 105th Cong., 1st sess., March 20, 1997.

S ince the early 1990s, some people who have very legitimate concerns about privacy, commerce, and computer security in the information age have argued that Government should simply stay out of the encryption issue entirely. Export controls have come in for particular criticism.

I want to make clear at the outset—because this is one of the areas where I think our position is misunderstood—that the Department of Justice and law enforcement in general supports the spread of strong encryption. We believe that the availability and wide use of strong cryptography are critical if the global information infrastructure is to fulfill its promise in areas such as personal communications, financial transactions, medical care, and a wide variety of other areas.

GOVERNMENT'S RESPONSIBILITIES

And our support for robust encryption stems in part from the fact that we have the responsibility under the law to protect privacy and commerce through a variety of statutes. At the same time, however, we also have the responsibility to protect the American people from the threats posed by terrorists, organized crime, child pornographers, drug cartels, foreign intelligence agents, and others, and to prosecute serious crime when it does occur.

And, thus, while we strongly favor the spread of strong encryption, we are gravely concerned that the proliferation and use of unbreakable encryption would seriously undermine the safety of the American people. Our national policy must reflect a balance between these competing interests of privacy and public safety.

If unbreakable encryption proliferates, critical law enforcement tools would be nullified. For example, even if the Government satisfies the rigorous legal and procedural requirements for obtaining an order to tap the phones of drug traffickers, the wiretap would be worthless if the intercepted communications amount to an unintelligible jumble of noises or symbols. Or we might legally seize the computer of a terrorist or a child molester using the Internet and be unable to read the data identifying his targets or his plans.

The potential harm to law enforcement and to our own security from unbreakable encryption could be devastating.

And I also want to emphasize that this concern is not a theoretical one or exaggerated. We are already encountering encryption in criminal investigations. As encryption proliferates and becomes an ordinary component of mass market items, and as the strength of encryption products increases, the threat to public safety will increase proportionately.

To some this is an acceptable outcome. They argue that people have a right to absolute immunity from Government intrusion regardless of the costs to public order and safety and that any new technology that enhances absolute privacy should go unrestricted.

A CAREFUL BALANCE

But our Founding Fathers recognized that an absolute right to privacy was incompatible with an ordered society, and so our Nation has never recognized such an absolute right. Rather, the fourth amendment strikes a careful balance between an individual's right to privacy and society's need, on appropriate occasions and when authorized by a court order, to intrude into that privacy. Our encryption policy should try to preserve that time-tested balance.

Others claim that our fears are overstated. They believe that with enough resources law enforcement and intelligence agencies can break any encryption. But that is just not true. The time and cost to decrypt a message rises exponentially as the length of the encryption key increases. To decrypt a single message using 56-bit data encryption standard (DES), which is a product whose export we are now allowing, would require over 1 year using a supercomputer, and it's never just one message.

Moreover, we're not talking only about Federal law enforcement here. We must also consider with the thousands of State and local police forces all over the country who don't have access to supercomputers. Brute force attacks are just not a feasible solution, particularly when what you're talking about is trying to find a kidnapped child before she's murdered or preventing a terrorist attack.

Our goal then is to encourage the use of strong encryption to protect privacy and commerce, but in a way that preserves law enforcement's ability to protect public safety and national security against terrorism and other threats. The best way to achieve this balance is through use of a key recovery system.

NO NEW POWERS

But I want to emphasize—because our position here is also often misunderstood—that a key recovery system would give the Government no new power. It would create no new authority to obtain data, to examine personal records or to eavesdrop. Access to encrypted data could be obtained only as part of a legally authorized investigation and under the same circumstances that today would authorize access to the unencrypted data. The same constitutional and statutory protections that preserve every

American's privacy interests today would prevent unauthorized intrusions in a key recovery regime. All that we would be doing is preserving law enforcement's ability to do what it is legally and constitutionally entitled to do today.

Technology Should Promote Public Safety

Without adequate legislation, law enforcement in the United States will be severely limited in its ability to combat the worst criminals and terrorists. Further, law enforcement agrees that the widespread use of robust non-key recovery encryption ultimately will devastate our ability to fight crime and prevent terrorism.

Simply stated, technology is rapidly developing to the point where powerful encryption will become commonplace both for routine telephone communications and for stored computer data. Without legislation that accommodates public safety and national security concerns, society's most dangerous criminals will be able to communicate safely and electronically store data without fear of discovery. Court orders to conduct electronic surveillance and court-authorized search warrants will be ineffectual, and the Fourth Amendment's carefully-struck balance between ensuring privacy and protecting public safety will be forever altered by technology. Technology should not dictate public policy, and it should promote, rather than defeat, public safety.

Janet Reno et al., Letter to Congress, July 18, 1997.

For many months we've been engaged in serious discussions on this subject with foreign governments, which are now anxious to join us in developing international standards to address this issue on a global scale. And we believe that key recovery encryption is going to become the worldwide standard. Thus, U.S. businesses will be able to compete abroad, effectively retaining and even expanding their market share, while law enforcement agencies continue to have a legally authorized means of decrypting encoded data.

The argument is sometimes made that key recovery encryption is not a solution because criminals will simply use nonkey recovery encryption to communicate among themselves and to hide evidence of their crimes. But we believe that if American companies develop and market strong key recovery encryption products and a global key management infrastructure arises, key recovery products will become the worldwide standard, and even criminals will use key recovery products, because even criminals need to communicate with legitimate organizations such as banks.

THE GENIE IS NOT OUT OF THE BOTTLE

We've heard, of course, the claim that the genie is out of the bottle—that strong encryption is already widely available overseas and its dissemination cannot be halted. We disagree with that.

First, although strong encryption products can be found overseas, these products are not ubiquitous, in part because of our export controls.

Second, the products that are available overseas are not widely used because there's not yet an infrastructure to support the distribution of keys among users.

Third, the quality of encryption products offered abroad varies greatly, with some encryption products not providing the level of protection advertised.

And, finally, the vast majority of legitimate businesses and individuals with a need for strong encryption do not and will not rely on encryption downloaded from the Internet from untested sources, but prefer to deal with known and reliable suppliers. For these reasons, export controls continue to serve an important function.

EXPORT CONTROLS

Now I want to make two other points about export controls. Our allies agree with us that unrestricted export of encryption would severely hamper law enforcement objectives. It would be a terrible irony if this Government, which prides itself on its leadership in fighting international crime, were to enact a law that our allies would perceive as jeopardizing public safety and weakening law enforcement agencies worldwide.

Second, in light of the concern that other countries have, we believe that many of these countries would respond to any lifting of U.S. export controls by imposing their own import controls or restricting the use of strong encryption by their citizens. Indeed, many countries are already doing so. In the long run, then, U.S. companies might well be not any better off if our export controls were lifted.

In light of these factors, we believe it would be profoundly unwise simply to lift export controls on encryption. National and domestic security should not be sacrificed for the sake of uncertain commercial benefits, especially when we have the real possibility of satisfying both security and commercial needs simultaneously.

Our policy in this area has to be a balanced one that recognizes and accommodates the competing interests of privacy and security. As I've said, law enforcement recognizes the privacy interests and endorses them, and we welcome strong encryption, and we've made many accommodations in our preferred policy in order to try to obtain the benefits of privacy while preserving law enforcement equities.

"[The government's insistence on reading any computer file] would open ... confidential personal data ... to unwarranted governmental interception, search and seizure."

COMPUTER ENCRYPTION CODES ARE NECESSARY TO PROTECT PRIVACY

Part I: Peter Wayner, Part II: James P. Lucier

Many individuals and businesses encode their computer files and transmissions to protect their privacy. Some lawmakers wish to require computer makers to provide the government with keys for decoding encrypted messages. In Part I of the following two-part viewpoint, Peter Wayner contends that the Framers of the Constitution knew that cryptography could stymie legal authorities and yet did not forbid it. In Part II, James P. Lucier argues that computer manufacturers must not be forced to turn their encryption code keys over to the government. Such an action would be a violation of the right to privacy, he asserts. Wayner is the author of *Disappearing Cryptography*. Lucier is the director of economic research at Americans for Tax Reform, a grassroots taxpayers' movement.

As you read, consider the following questions:

1. What evidence does Wayner present to support his assertion that the Framers of the Constitution were familiar with cryptography?
2. What is the key escrow encryption system, according to Lucier?
3. In Lucier's opinion, how is the government forcing the American computer industry to accept the key escrow encryption system?

Part I: Reprinted from Peter Wayner, "Giving Away Secrets," *The New York Times*, July 29, 1997, by permission. Copyright ©1997 by The New York Times Company. Part II: Reprinted from James P. Lucier, "The Government's Magic Key," *The Washington Times*, December 5, 1995, by permission of *The Washington Times*.

I

Internet hype can turn age-old problems into new grave threats. The biggest tempest may be the concern over the use of encryption, or secret codes, to scramble information sent over the Internet and other computer networks. The use of codes may thrill people who want to protect the business plans on their office computers and the love letters they send by E-mail. But it worries the Director of the Federal Bureau of Investigation, Louis J. Freeh, and other law-enforcement officials.

Mr. Freeh is right to be concerned that encryption can limit the ability of law enforcement to gather electronic evidence from wiretaps and court-ordered searches. But he was wrong when he told the Senate Judiciary Committee that "technology and telecommunications well beyond the contemplation of the Framers" will bring "a terrible upset of the balance so wisely set forth in the Fourth Amendment." In other words, he envisions the balance tipping against the police, because they will have more difficulty conducting reasonable searches if more of the information they are seeking is encrypted.

CRYPTOGRAPHY IS NOT NEW

Yet cryptography wasn't beyond the contemplation of the Framers, because many of them were skilled code makers and code breakers themselves. David Kahn's book *The Codebreakers* tells how codes have affected history for more than 3,000 years. According to Mr. Kahn, George Washington had to deal with the problem when a coded message was intercepted in August 1775 from Benjamin Church, a member of the Massachusetts Congress who was a spy for the British. The message, which was finally deciphered, told the English details of American troop movements.

As Mr. Kahn reveals, both sides in the Revolutionary War made extensive use of encryption. Benedict Arnold designed the complex code that he used to sell out his country. James Lovell of the Continental Congress helped win the war by breaking the codes used by General Cornwallis. After the war, Thomas Jefferson and James Madison communicated in their own private code. And Benjamin Franklin devised his own cipher for sending dispatches from Europe.

Yet in writing the Bill of Rights, the Founders did not forbid cryptography, even though they knew how powerful a tool it could be. Nor did they suggest that the police be able to obtain the plain text of a coded message. But that could happen under a measure sponsored by Senator Bob Kerrey of Nebraska, a Democrat, and Senator John McCain of Arizona, a Republican. Under their bill, the key to any code used to scramble information sent on the Internet would have to be given to the proper authorities. The Clinton Administration supports similar measures. [No action had been taken on this bill as of March 1998.]

CREATIVE CRIMINALS

James Bamford, in *The Puzzle Palace,* describes how the F.B.I. broke the case of the gangsters who were communicating without phone calls or letters. Agents discovered that the gangsters sent their shirts to Las Vegas to be dry cleaned—and that the number of shirts held the coded message. No ban on cryptography on the Internet will be able to thwart creative crooks like these, but diligent police work can find cracks in the armor. This is why the National Research Council has recommended that Congress invest in research to help the F.B.I. better understand computers and codes.

The F.B.I. faces a daunting task. Encryption makes it impossible for agents to gather all the evidence they would like. But the answer is not to regulate, and in effect destroy, the use of coded messages. Criminals would probably find a way around the rules, and the rest of us could lose a powerful tool for protecting our privacy.

II

George Orwell predicted that "Big Brother" would be watching us by the mid-80s. Although futurists warned of government entities controlling communications vehicles and using them to infringe on individual citizen rights, to most the concept of a Big Brother government was just a fictional vision of the future.

THE THREAT TO INDIVIDUAL PRIVACY

Well, Orwell was right. He was just a decade early. Now at the dawn of the "new information age," that threat has turned into reality. Databases filled with private and personal information abound, government experts are discussing how best to design a national identification card and what type of information it should contain, and the Clinton administration is trying to insist on the ability to read any computer file and decode any electronic file transmitted.

Although all of this personal invasion is cause for concern, the most immediately troubling is the government's effort to limit citizens' ability to protect personal and professional information over digital networks. If allowed, such an action would open American citizens' and businesses' confidential personal data and valuable proprietary information to unwarranted governmental interception, search and seizure. Law enforcement officials and FBI agents will be able to obtain access to financial transactions and personal correspondence. It's government intervention at its finest—an electronic Ruby Ridge.

THE KEY ESCROW ENCRYPTION SYSTEM

The Clinton administration has circulated a proposal that would effectively force all computer hardware and software manufacturers to produce encryption products that contain a key that would unlock encoded information to government officials. Known as "key escrow encryption system," this encryption technology would allow for unlimited government surveillance.

The administration is using the desire of America's computing industries to develop and sell their programs worldwide to leverage its demands for a feature that will permit government access to encrypted information. Essentially, the administration threatens to classify any software product that is secure from government snooping as a controlled export item subject to the same constraints that limit sales of military hardware and defense production equipment. This effectively kills any hope of export sales. Furthermore, administration officials have threatened to seek legislation making it mandatory if American companies do not "voluntarily" include key escrow.

A SECURE IDENTITY

Public key encryption—a method for making virtually unbreakable codes using complementary encoding keys, one public and the other private—has two crucial but sometimes contradictory capabilities: securing communications and establishing identity. Security agencies such as the FBI and the National Security Agency (NSA), which make their livings in large part from listening to other people's conversations, are encouraging governments to keep the full strength of public key encryption (indeed, encryption of all kinds) out of the hands of private citizens. But the same technology is crucial to creating "unbreakable" identities in cyberspace—the certain knowledge of who is who. Thus, any compromise of people's ability to control their communications also undermines their control of their own digital identities: Is that your signature? Or some dishonest dog's? And that uncertainty in turn undermines the notions of commitment and responsibility that are fundamental to lawful commerce.

John Browning, *Wired*, November 1997.

Yet millions of consumers are rejecting this technology, preferring to purchase products that provide strong encryption capabilities that are not easily unlocked by government officials. Although consumer demands for encryption capabilities are clear, they have expressed no desire for government-controlled key escrow systems, which they see as unwarranted and undesirable.

Government officials defend key escrow by arguing that strong encryption may be a threat to national security. This is a great misunderstanding of consumer demands and the technology that is already widely available. There are hundreds of foreign products manufactured by scores of foreign companies. Of course, non-key escrow encryption programs also are readily available in thousands of U.S. retail stores and, despite U.S. laws prohibiting export, are easily transferred abroad with a modem and a public telephone line.

GREATER GOVERNMENT RESTRICTIONS

The failure of government policy to keep up with technological innovations restricts the ability of computer users in the United States and abroad to use encryption to protect their personal and proprietary information at home and in business. Not only will such a policy hinder the continued growth and future success of the U.S. software industry, one of this nation's most competitive and fastest growing industries, it will set the standard of government intervention and restriction in the computer era. Look no farther than the reports of a French hacker who broke Netscape's codes to see the need for stronger encryption for American companies to produce secure products for the global marketplace.

Resolving the encryption export issue is critical to the future of the computing and communications industries. With businesses and consumers becoming increasingly dependent on the Internet for the transmission of confidential information, administration export restrictions are placing U.S. businesses and American consumers at a disadvantage to foreign counterparts.

Rather than embracing new technologies and moving into a new era, the federal government is negatively responding the only way it knows how—through control and manipulation. Rather than considering citizens' privacy and protection issues, the Clinton administration is trying to tighten control on technologies that would protect the private communications of millions of cyberspace consumers. Rather than working with industry to understand the dynamism of the marketplace, the government is establishing imprecise limitations for undefined problems. In short, the administration's "new" encryption policy appears to be little more than a front for greater government restrictions.

THE GOVERNMENT VERSUS THE AVERAGE CITIZEN

Both current and proposed government policies are already outdated. The technology genie is out of the bottle. The Clinton administration's attempt to restrict encryption is simply a backdoor policy serving government's interests against the needs of the average citizen. As consumers and businesses move to acquire software that will provide critical links to the Internet and networked environments, industry must have the freedom to develop products with encryption capabilities that meet consumer demands for privacy protection in the United States and abroad.

PERIODICAL BIBLIOGRAPHY

The following articles have been selected to supplement the diverse views presented in this chapter. Addresses are provided for periodicals not indexed in the *Readers' Guide to Periodical Literature*, the *Alternative Press Index*, the *Social Sciences Index*, or the *Index to Legal Periodicals and Books*.

David Banisar and Simon Davies
"The Code War," *Index on Censorship*, January/February 1998.

Ann Beeson
"Should the Internet Be Regulated? Openness Should Be Preserved," *World & I*, February 1998. Available from 25 Beacon St., Boston, MA 02108-2803.

Ann Beeson
"Top Ten Threats to Civil Liberties in Cyberspace," *Human Rights*, Spring 1996. Available from 750 N. Lake Shore Dr., Chicago, IL 60611.

David Brin
"The Transparent Society," *Wired*, December 1996. Available from PO Box 191826, San Francisco, CA 94119-9866.

David Gelernter
"Free Speech and the Net," *Weekly Standard*, May 12, 1997. Available from PO Box 96153, Washington, DC 20090-6153.

Amy Harmon
"The Self-Appointed Cops of the Information Age," *New York Times*, December 7, 1997.

Joshua Micah Marshall
"Will Free Speech Get Tangled in the Net?" *American Prospect*, January/February 1998.

Andrew L. Shapiro
"Privacy for Sale," *Nation*, June 23, 1997.

Glenn Simpson
"Internet Users Spooked About Spies' New Role," *Wall Street Journal*, October 2, 1995.

Rebecca Vesely
"The Generation Gap," *Wired*, October 1997.

Thomas E. Weber
"Browsers Beware: The Web Is Watching," *Wall Street Journal*, June 27, 1996.

FOR FURTHER DISCUSSION

CHAPTER 1

1. Richard Delgado and David Yun argue that hate speech condemns the persecuted to second-class status. How does the American Civil Liberties Union respond to this concern? Whose argument is strongest? Give examples from the viewpoints to support your answer.

2. Richard Parker contends that burning the American flag as a form of protest shows extreme disrespect for the United States and must be outlawed. Roger Pilon and Carole Shields agree that flag burning is offensive, but they argue that it must be protected because it is a form of political speech. Based on the authors' arguments, do you believe flag burning is a form of political speech that should be protected? Why or why not? Explain your answer.

3. Catherine Itzin asserts that pornography should be illegal because it harms and degrades women. Nadine Strossen maintains, however, that a ban on pornography would lead to restrictions on other forms of offensive speech. How do Itzin's and Strossen's differing views on pornography reflect their beliefs about free speech?

CHAPTER 2

1. Amitai Etzioni maintains that a reduction in privacy benefits society because it exposes criminals to public scrutiny. In Joseph S. Fulda's opinion, however, a loss of privacy threatens a society's freedom. Which author makes a stronger case? Support your answer with examples from the viewpoints.

2. Cass R. Sunstein offers several examples of laws that could be passed to protect the privacy of celebrities. Do Sunstein's recommendations convince you that more laws are needed to protect an individual's privacy? Why or why not? How does Jane E. Kirtley respond to these suggestions? Which argument is strongest? Explain your answer.

3. Antonin Scalia and his colleagues argue that because student-athletes have a lesser expectation of privacy, random drug testing does not violate their right to privacy. Sandra Day O'Connor, John Paul Stevens, and David Souter contend that testing student-athletes for drugs violates their right to privacy unless the tests are based on a reasonable suspicion of wrongdoing. Based on your reading of the viewpoints, do you think random drug testing of student-athletes violates

their right to privacy? Support your answer with examples from the viewpoints.

CHAPTER 3

1. Linda Bowles asserts that the wishes of the majority who favor prayer in schools are overridden by the minority who do not. Roger Simon argues that the rights of the minority who do not want prayer in school will be violated if the majority insists on imposing its will on them. Based on your reading of the viewpoints, do you think the majority's wishes should be overruled by the rights of the minority? In your opinion, is a moment of silence an acceptable compromise? Why or why not?

2. Bob Peterson maintains that using publicly funded vouchers to send schoolchildren to private religious schools takes away tax dollars needed for public education. Denis P. Doyle argues that Catholic schools cannot survive without school vouchers. Whose argument is stronger? In your opinion, should public funds be used to send children to private religious schools? Support your answers with examples from the viewpoints.

CHAPTER 4

1. Nathaniel Sheppard Jr. warns that computer users can expect their activities to be monitored while they are surfing the Internet. How does Joseph Burns respond to these concerns? Based on your reading of the viewpoints, do you think the Internet threatens the right to privacy? Explain your answer.

2. Shyla Welch contends that the ease with which children can find and view pornography on the Internet requires that steps be taken to protect them. The American Civil Liberties Union maintains, however, that such protections would constitute censorship and violate the right of free speech. What evidence does each of their viewpoints offer to support these arguments? Which argument seems stronger? Why?

ORGANIZATIONS TO CONTACT

The editors have compiled the following list of organizations concerned with the issues debated in this book. The descriptions are derived from materials provided by the organizations. All have publications or information available for interested readers. The list was compiled on the date of publication of the present volume; the information provided here may change. Be aware that many organizations take several weeks or longer to respond to inquiries, so allow as much time as possible.

American Civil Liberties Union (ACLU)
125 Broad St., 18th Fl., New York, NY 10004-2400
(212) 549-2500
e-mail: aclu@aclu.org • web address: http://www.aclu.org
The ACLU is a national organization that works to defend civil rights as guaranteed in the Constitution. It publishes various materials on civil liberties, including the report *Restoring Civil Liberties: A Blueprint for Action for the Clinton Administration*, the triannual newsletter *Civil Liberties*, and a set of handbooks on individual rights.

Americans United for Separation of Church and State (AUSCS)
1816 Jefferson Pl. NW, Washington, DC 20036
(202) 466-3234 • fax: (202) 466-2587
e-mail: americansunited@au.org • web address: http://www.au.org
AUSCS works to protect religious freedom for all Americans. Its principal means of action are litigation, education, and advocacy. It opposes the passing of either federal or state laws that threaten the separation of church and state. Its publications include brochures, pamphlets, and the monthly newsletter *Church and State*.

Center for Democracy and Technology (CDT)
1001 G St. NW, Suite 700E, Washington, DC 20001
(202) 637-9800 • fax: (202) 637-0968
e-mail: webmaster@cdt.org • web address: http://www.cdt.org
CDT's mission is to develop public policy solutions that advance constitutional civil liberties and democratic values in new computer and communications media. Its publications include issue briefs, policy papers, and *CDT Policy Posts*, an on-line publication that covers issues regarding the civil liberties of people using the information highway.

The Heritage Foundation
214 Massachusetts Ave. NE, Washington, DC 20002-4999
(800) 544-4843 • (202) 546-4400 • fax: (202) 544-2260
e-mail: pubs@heritage.org • web address: http://www.heritage.org
The foundation is a conservative public policy organization dedicated to free-market principles, individual liberty, and limited government. It favors limiting freedom of the press when that freedom threatens national security. Its resident scholars publish position papers on a

wide range of issues through publications such as the weekly *Back-grounder* and the quarterly *Policy Review*.

Human Rights Watch
350 Fifth Ave., 34th Fl., New York, NY 10118
(212) 290-4700
e-mail: hrwnyc@hrw.org • web address: http://www.hrw.org

Human Rights Watch regularly investigates human rights abuses in over seventy countries around the world. It promotes civil liberties and defends freedom of thought, due process, and equal protection of the law. Its goal is to hold governments accountable for human rights violations they may commit against individuals because of their political, ethnic, or religious affiliations. It publishes the *Human Rights Watch Quarterly Newsletter*, the annual *Human Rights Watch World Report*, and a semiannual publications catalog.

Institute for a Drug-Free Workplace
1225 I St. NW, Suite 1000, Washington, DC 20005-3914
(202) 842-7400 • fax: (202) 842-0022
e-mail: dgrecich@drugfreeworkplace.org
web address: http://www.drugfreeworkplace.org

The institute is dedicated to preserving the rights of employers and employees who participate in substance abuse prevention programs and to positively influencing the national debate on the issue of drug abuse in the workplace. It publishes the *Guide to Dangerous Drugs*, the pamphlets *What Every Employee Should Know About Drug Abuse: Answers to 20 Good Questions* and *Does Drug Testing Work?* as well as several fact sheets.

Lindesmith Center
400 W. 59th St., New York, NY 10019
(212) 548-0695 • fax: (212) 548-4670
e-mail: lindesmith@sorosny.org
web address: http://www.lindesmith.org

The Lindesmith Center is a policy research institute that focuses on broadening the debate on drug policy and related issues. The center houses a library and information center; acts as a link between scholars, government, and the media; and undertakes projects on special topics such as methadone policy reform and alternatives to drug testing in the workplace. The center publishes fact sheets on a variety of topics as well as the report *An Evaluation of Fitness-for-Duty Testing*.

National Coalition Against Censorship (NCAC)
275 Seventh Ave., New York, NY 10001
(212) 807-6222 • fax: (212) 807-6245
e-mail: ncac@ncac.org • web address: http://www.ncac.org

NCAC is an alliance of organizations committed to defending freedom of thought, inquiry, and expression by engaging in public education and advocacy on national and local levels. It publishes periodic reports and the quarterly *Censorship News*.

National Coalition Against Pornography (N-CAP)
800 Compton Rd., Suite 9224, Cincinnati, OH 45231-9964
(513) 521-6227 • fax: (513) 521-6337
web address: www.nationalcoalition.org
N-CAP is an organization of business, religious, and civic leaders who work to eliminate pornography. Because it believes a link exists between pornography and violence, N-CAP encourages citizens to support the enforcement of obscenity laws and to close down pornography outlets in their neighborhoods. Publications include the books *Final Report of the Attorney General's Commission on Pornography*, *The Mind Polluters*, and *Pornography: A Human Tragedy*.

People for the American Way Foundation (PFAW)
2000 M St. NW, Suite 400, Washington, DC 20036
(202) 467-4999 • (202) 293-2672
e-mail: pfaw@pfaw.org • web address: http://www.pfaw.org
PFAW works to increase tolerance and respect for America's diverse cultures, religions, and values. It distributes educational materials, leaflets, and brochures, including the reports *A Right Wing and a Prayer: The Religious Right in Your Public Schools* and *Attacks on the Freedom to Learn*.

Religion in Public Education Resource Center (RPERC)
5 County Center Dr., Oroville, CA 95965
(916) 538-7847 • fax: (916) 538-7846
e-mail: bbenoit@edison.bcoe.butte.k12.ca.us
web address: http://www.csuchico.edu/rs/reperc.html
The center believes religion should be studied in public schools in ways that do not promote the values or beliefs of one religion over another but that expose students to such beliefs. It publishes the triannual magazine *Religion and Public Education* and resource materials for teachers and administrators.

Rockford Institute Center on Religion and Society
934 N. Main St., Rockford, IL 61103
(815) 964-5053 • fax: (815) 965-1826
e-mail: rkfdinst@bossnt.com
The center is a research and educational organization that advocates a more public role for religion and religious values in American life. It publishes the quarterly *This World: A Journal of Religion and Public Life* and the monthly *Religion and Society Report*.

BIBLIOGRAPHY OF BOOKS

Ellen Alderman and
Caroline Kennedy

The Right to Privacy. New York: Knopf, 1995.

Anne Wells Branscomb

Who Owns Information?: From Privacy to Public Access.
New York: BasicBooks, 1994.

Ann Cavoukian
and Don Tapscott

*Who Knows: Safeguarding Your Privacy in a Networked
World.* New York: McGraw-Hill, 1997.

J.M. Coetzee

Giving Offense: Essays on Censorship. Chicago: University of Chicago Press, 1996.

Richard Delgado
and Jean Stefancic

*Must We Defend Nazis? Hate Speech, Pornography, and the
New First Amendment.* New York: New York University Press, 1997.

Richard Dooling

Blue Streak: Swearing, Free Speech, and Sexual Harassment.
New York: Random House, 1996.

Stanley Eugene Fish

*There's No Such Thing as Free Speech, and It's a Good Thing,
Too.* New York: Oxford University Press, 1994.

Owen M. Fiss

The Irony of Free Speech. Cambridge, MA: Harvard
University Press, 1996.

Ronald B. Flowers

*That Godless Court?: Supreme Court Decisions on Church-
State Relationships.* Louisville, KY: Westminster John
Knox Press, 1994.

Marvin E. Frankel

Faith and Freedom: Religious Liberty in America. New
York: Hill and Wang, 1994.

Robert Justin Goldstein

*Burning the Flag: The Great 1989–1990 American Flag
Desecration Controversy.* Kent, OH: Kent State University Press, 1996.

Ted Gottfried

Privacy: Individual Right v. Social Needs. Brookfield, CT:
Millbrook Press, 1994.

Kent Greenawalt

*Fighting Words: Individuals, Communities, and Liberties of
Speech.* Princeton, NJ: Princeton University Press,
1995.

Rochelle Gurstein

*The Repeal of Reticence: A History of America's Cultural and
Legal Struggles over Free Speech, Obscenity, Sexual Liberation,
and Modern Art.* New York: Hill and Wang, 1996.

Milton Heumann,
Thomas W. Church, and
David P. Redlawsk, eds.

Hate Speech on Campus: Cases, Case Studies, and Commentary. Boston: Northeastern University Press, 1997.

Steven J. Heyman, ed.

Hate Speech and the Constitution. New York: Garland,
1996.

Gregg Ivers

*To Build a Wall: American Jews and the Separation of Church
and State.* Charlottesville: University Press of Virginia, 1995.

Brian Kahin and Charles Nesson, eds.

Borders in Cyberspace: Information Policy and the Global Information Infrastructure. Cambridge, MA: MIT Press, 1997.

Richard Klingler

The New Information Industry: Regulatory Challenges and the First Amendment. Washington, DC: Brookings Institution Press, 1996.

Isaac Kramnick and R. Laurence Moore

The Godless Constitution: The Case Against Religious Correctness. New York: Norton, 1996.

Gara LaMarche, ed.

Speech and Equality: Do We Really Have to Choose? New York: New York University Press, 1996.

Laura J. Lederer and Richard Delgado, eds.

The Price We Pay: The Case Against Racist Speech, Hate Propaganda, and Pornography. New York: Hill and Wang, 1995.

Leonard Williams Levy

The Establishment Clause: Religion and the First Amendment. Chapel Hill: University of North Carolina Press, 1994.

Barry W. Lynn, Marc D. Stein, and Oliver S. Thomas

The Right to Religious Liberty: The Basic ACLU Guide to Religious Rights. 2nd ed. Carbondale: Southern Illinois University Press, 1995.

Laurence R. Marcus

Fighting Words: The Politics of Hateful Speech. Westport, CT: Praeger, 1996.

Deckle McLean

Privacy and Its Invasion. Westport, CT: Praeger, 1995.

Darien A. McWhirter

Search, Seizure, and Privacy. Phoenix: Oryx Press, 1994.

Warren A. Nord

Religion and American Education: Rethinking a National Dilemma. Chapel Hill: University of North Carolina Press, 1995.

Bruce Schneier and David Banisar, eds.

The Electronic Privacy Papers: Documents on the Battle for Privacy in the Age of Surveillance. New York: John Wiley, 1997.

Gini Graham Scott

Mind Your Own Business: The Battle for Personal Privacy. New York: Plenum Press, 1995.

Nadine Strossen

Defending Pornography: Free Speech, Sex, and the Fight for Women's Rights. New York: Scribner, 1995.

Samuel Walker

Hate Speech: The History of an American Controversy. Lincoln: University of Nebraska Press, 1994.

Rita Kirk Whillock and David Slayden, eds.

Hate Speech. Thousand Oaks, CA: Sage Publications, 1995.

Nicholas Wolfson

Hate Speech, Sex Speech, Free Speech. Westport, CT: Praeger, 1997.

INDEX

Acton, James, 92, 103, 104
Adams, Samuel, 131
Administrative Office of the United
  States Courts, 109
African Americans, 31, 33, 34, 154
  and conservative politicians, 150-51
  drop in college enrollment among, 28
America, 79
American Academy of Pediatrics, 94
American Bar Association, 56
American Civil Liberties Union
  (ACLU), 35, 36, 144, 174
  director of, 107
  on free speech, 24
  president of, 65
American Civil Rights Institute, 150
American Library Association (ALA), 18
Americans for Tax Reform, 189
Americans United for Separation of
  Church and State, 123
America Online, 181
Ameritech Corp., 164
antiterrorism act, 108, 109
Arizona, 42, 191
Arizona v. Hicks, 102
Arnn, Larry P., 64, 144
Arnold, Benedict, 190
Augustine of Hippo, Saint, 122

Bacard, Andre, 164
Backus, Isaac, 125, 126
Bakker, Jim, 139
Baptist Joint Committee on Public
  Affairs, 120
Baptists, 55, 124-26
Barnes, Robin D., 34
Barton, David, 140, 141
Bell Curve, The (Herrnstein and Murray),
  150
Berger, Raoul, 134
Bible, 54, 129, 131, 132, 154
  Catholic/Protestant preferred versions
  of, 155
Biggers, Neal, 143
Black, Hugo, 129, 130
Blaine, James G., 155
Bolick, Clint, 149, 150
Bovard, James, 20
Bowles, Linda, 142
Bradbury, Ray, 175
Bradley Foundation, 149, 150
Brandeis, Louis, 86
Braveheart (movie), 24
Brennan, William, 49
Breyer, Stephen, 89

Browning, John, 192
Brown v. Board of Education, 150
Burns, Joseph, 166

California, 20, 87, 144, 150
Calvin, John, 123
Canada, 62
Canavan, Francis, 64
Catholic schools, 154, 155, 156-57
censorship, 60, 63
  condemned by American Library
  Association, 18
  of Internet
    is necessary, 169-70
      for protection of children,
      171-72, 173
    long-term implications of, 175,
    176-77
    and rating system problems, 179-80
    as violation of free speech, 17,
    180-82
    according to Supreme Court,
    177-78
  should be avoided, 67-68, 69
  see also free speech
child abuse, 75
  see also pornography
Chiles, Lawton, 143
China, 57
Christian Science Monitor, 75, 181
Chronicle of Higher Education, 28
Churchill, Sir Winston, 54
City College, New York, 43
City of God, The (Augustine), 122
Claremont Institute, 144
Clinton administration, 191, 193, 194
CNN, 167
Codebreakers, The (Kahn), 190
Coleman, James, 154
college campuses, 28, 34, 37, 39
  and speech codes, 40-43
Colorado, 150
computer encryption
  and export controls, 184, 187, 192,
  193
  and history of code use, 190
  makes law enforcement difficult,
  191
  as protection of privacy, 189, 192
  prevents government surveillance,
  194
  as threat to safety, 183-86
  is more compelling than right to
  privacy, 188
Connecticut, 130

Constantine (Roman emperor), 122-23
Court of Appeals, U.S., 92, 94, 96
crime, 75, 191
  see also pornography; wiretaps
Critical Path Aids Project, 178
Curran, John Philpot, 23

data encryption standard (DES), 185
Delaware v. Prouse, 93
Delgado, Richard, 27, 34
Diana, princess of Wales, 81, 82, 85,
  86, 88
Digital Telephony and Communications
  Privacy Improvement Act, 113
Direct Marketing Association (DMA),
  80
Disappearing Cryptography (Wayner), 189
District Court of Vernonia, Oregon, 92,
  93, 96, 104
Dover, Kenneth J., 35
Doyle, Denis P., 153
drug problems in schools, 90, 96-97
  and Student Athlete Drug Policy
  proposal, 91-92
Dworkin, Andrea, 62, 63, 67, 68

e-mail, 190
Edison Project, 157
Ehrenreich, Barbara, 51
Eleven Myths About Church and State
  (Americans United for Separation of
  Church and State), 123
Elkins v. United States, 92
Emancipating School Prayer (Jaffa), 144
Endangered Species Act, 115
England. See United Kingdom
EPIC (Electronic Privacy Information
  Center), 80
Etzioni, Amitai, 73
Evans, M. Stanton, 128

Fahrenheit 451 (Bradbury), 175
FBI (Federal Bureau of Investigation),
  31, 190, 191, 192
  and computer hackers, 163, 193
  and wiretapping, 107, 108, 109, 110,
  111
Federal Communications Decency Act
  (CDA), 175, 177, 178, 182
Federal Register, 79, 108
First Baptist Church of Providence, 125
flag burning, 40, 139
  restrictions on
    are appropriate, 44, 45
      because flag symbolizes
      Constitution, 46-47, 51
    opposed by majority of Americans,
    56, 58

undermine political freedom,
  52-55, 57
  con, 48-50
  see also hate speech laws
Florida, 75, 145
France, 87
Francis, Mike, 168
Franklin, Benjamin, 54, 190
free speech, 28
  and freedom of press, 82
  as indivisible right, 38
  as more than political tool, 23
  and pornography, 62
  restriction of, 17-21, 60, 63
    is inappropriate, 22-26, 67-68, 69
      because it leads to ignorance, 24
      because moral virtue cannot be
      compelled, 25
  sexual expression is part of, 66
  tolerated exceptions to protection of,
  33
  see also censorship; flag burning; hate
  speech laws
"Freedom of Expression" (ACLU), 24
Freeh, Louis, 108, 109, 190
Fried, Charles, 46
Friedman, Milton, 150
Fulda, Joseph S., 77

Gaouette, Nicole, 75
Gelernter, David, 112
Gibson, Mel, 24
Gingrich, Newt, 140
Ginsburg, Ruth Bader, 89
Glasser, Ira, 43, 148
Goldstein, Robert Justin, 57
Golle, John, 157, 158
Goss v. Lopez, 102
Gottfried, Paul, 42
Graglia, Lino, 134
Grant, Ulysses S., 155
Great Britain. See United Kingdom
Greenberg, Paul, 47
Greene, Linda S., 30
Grey, Anthony, 68
Griffin v. Wisconsin, 93
Guardian, 62
gun control, 115

Hall, Radclyffe, 60
hate speech laws
  are necessary, 27
    only when conduct harasses
    individual, 41-42
    to protect minorities, 31, 32, 33
    as response to increase in hate
    crime, 28, 37
  First Amendment rights threatened

by, 38-40, 42-43
ineffectiveness of, 36, 40-41
poor arguments against, 30-34
and paternalism, 29, 33, 35
rejected by Supreme Court, 67-68
Hawley, Richard A., 96
Henry VIII (king of England), 123
Hentoff, Nat, 33, 49, 50
Herring, Mark Y., 17
Higginbotham, Paul, 151
Holmes, Oliver Wendell, 67
homosexuality, 60
Hyde, Henry J., 114

IBM, 176
Illinois, 144, 164
Illinois v. Krull, 99
immigration bill, 108
Indianapolis city council, 62
Ingraham v. Wright, 102
Insight magazine, 42
Institute for Justice, 149
Intellectual Freedom Manual (American
    Library Association), 18
Internal Revenue Service (IRS), 79, 80,
    115
Internet, 18, 19, 184, 190, 191
cybersex on, 20
as threat to privacy, 162-65
is exaggerated, 166-68
see also censorship
Ireland, Pat, 18
Itzin, Catherine, 59

Jackson, Robert, 56
Jaffa, Harry V., 144, 145
Jasna, Robert, 152
Jefferson, Thomas, 20, 126, 136, 190
and religion clauses in Constitution,
    129
on separation of church and state, 123
Joyce, Michael, 149

Kaczynski, Ted, 112
Kahn, David, 190
Keillor, Garrison, 66
Kennedy, Anthony, 89
Kennedy, Ted, 18
Kerrey, Bob, 190
key escrow encryption system, 192, 193
Kilpatrick, James K., 93
King, Martin Luther, Jr., 31, 32
Kirtley, Jane E., 85
Kozol, Jonathan, 152
Kristol, Irving, 18
Kuromiya, Kiyoshi, 178-79

Landmark Legal Foundation, 150

Lederer, Laura J., 34
Lefevre, Greg, 167
Leland, John, 125-26
Letter to Congress (Reno et al.), 186
Limbaugh, Rush, 18
Lippmann, Walter, 20
Li-Ron, Yael, 167
Litt, Robert S., 183
Locke, John, 20
Lost Rights (Bovard), 20
Lucier, James P., 191

MacKinnon, Catharine, 62, 63, 67, 68
Madison, James, 123, 129, 136, 190
and amendments to Constitution,
    132-33
certain views of dismissed by
    Supreme Court, 135
and influence of John Leland, 126
Madonna, 66
Mann, Horace, 156
Mapplethorpe, Robert, 66
Marchiano, Linda, 61
Marshall, John, 50
Maryland, 164
constitution of, 131
Massachusetts, 124, 125, 130, 131
McCain, John, 191
McClellan, James, 134
McCurley, Virginia, 181
Megan's law, 75
Memorial and Remonstrance (Madison), 123
Microsoft, 176, 179
Mill, John Stuart, 20, 23, 24
Milton, John, 20
Milwaukee Journal Sentinel, 149
Minneapolis City Council, 61, 62, 63
minorities, 31
Mississippi, 143, 145
Mitnick, Kevin, 163, 164
Montesquieu, Baron de, 20
Moral Ideas for America (Arnn and Jeffrey),
    64
Motion Picture Association of America
    (MPAA), 180
Murphy, Laura W., 107
Murray, Charles, 149-50
Murray, Patty, 176

National Forum, 30
National Institute Against Prejudice and
    Violence, 28, 31
National Journalist Center, 128
National Organization for Women, 18
National Research Council, 191
National Security Agency (NSA), 192
Nebraska, 190
Neier, Aryeh, 38

New England, 130, 154
New Hampshire, 130, 131
New Jersey, 131
New Jersey v. T.L.O., 92, 105
    and exception made for school-
    children, 102
    school search approved in, 93-94
    because of reasonable suspicion, 100
New Testament, 121, 122, 127
New York, 130
New York World's Fair (1939), 115
New Zealand, 62
Northwest Ordinance, 132

O'Connell, Donald, 164
O'Connor, Sandra Day, 98
Oklahoma, 19
Oklahoma City bombing, 109
Ombudsperson Office Law, 76
On Liberty (Mill), 23
Oregon, 150
    constitution of, 92
Orwell, George, 191

paparazzi, 85, 86
Parker, Richard, 44
Partners Advancing Values in Education,
    149
paternalism, 29, 33, 35
PC Magazine, 167
Penthouse magazine, 172
People for the American Way, 55
Perkins, Joseph, 83
Peter Hart poll, 56
Peterson, Bob, 146
Peterson, Paul E., 155
Philadelphia, 125
Phillips, Wendell, 126
Pilon, Roger, 52
Platform for Internet Content Selection
    (PICS), 176, 177, 179
Playboy magazine, 172
pornography, 170-71, 172
    should be restricted
    on basis of harm, not obscenity,
        63-64
    should not be restricted, 65-69
    because of constitutional right to
        free speech, 66-68
    women and children harmed/
        objectified by, 60, 61-62
Powell, Colin, 50, 150
Powell, Lewis, 105
prayer in public schools, 129, 135
    is unnecessary, 139
    public support for, 143
    as threat to religious freedom, 138,
        140-41

see also religious freedom; religious
    schools
Price We Pay: The Case Against Racist Speech,
    Hate Propaganda, and Pornography, The
    (Barnes), 34
privacy
    definition of, 86
    from government intrusion, 185,
        191-92, 194
    is not absolute value, 76, 185
    is protected by free market, 80
    laws to protect
        ineffectiveness of, 86-87
        necessity for more, 81-84
        to prevent harassment of
            celebrities, 82-83
        violation of First Amendment, 85, 88
    loss of
        is beneficial to society, 73-76
        is harmful to society, 77
        right to, 78
    tax system violates, 78-79
    see also computer encryption; Internet;
        random drug tests; wiretaps
Privacy Act (1974), 80
Protestant Reformation, 123
Protestant religion, 130
Protestant schools, 154-55
Providence Plantation, 125
Puzzle Palace, The (Bamford), 191

Race Relations Act (U.K.), 40, 63
racism, 30, 32, 35
    and hate crimes, 31
    and hate speech, 29, 34
    and pornography, 63
random drug tests, 92
    do not violate privacy rights, 89, 97
    when motivated by children's best
        interests, 94-96
    and monitoring of urine samples, 76,
        91, 100
    reasons for, 90, 93
    violate right to privacy, 98-99
    as defined by Constitution, 100,
        102, 106
    as ineffective against school drug
        problems, 101, 104, 105
    as negative message for children, 103
Recreational Software Advisory Council
    (RSAC), 176, 180
Rehnquist, William, 89
religious freedom, 121
    and Baptist leaders, 124
    prohibition of school prayer a threat
        to, 142-45
    see also prayer in public schools;
        separation of church and state

religious schools
  tax money should fund, 153
    according to conservatives, 149-50
    to increase availability of private
      education, 155, 157-58
    because of popularity of private
      schools, 154
  tax money should not fund, 146-47,
    151-52
    because of corrupt administration,
      148
    because of lack of accountability, 149
    because of voter resistance to
      voucher system, 150
  see also Catholic schools
Reno, Janet, 186
Republican Party, 150
Rhode Island, 125
Ruby Ridge incident, 109, 192

San Diego North County Times, 114
San Diego Union-Tribune, 47, 83, 148
  ComputerLink, 168
Scalia, Antonin, 89
Scholastic Aptitude Test, 140
schools, Catholic, 154, 155, 156-57
school-voucher programs. See religious
  schools
separation of church and state, 121-23
  anti-Catholic origins of, 154-55, 156,
    158
  and Baptist leaders, 124-26
  Constitution's framers intended, 120,
    124, 127
    con, 128-29, 130, 133, 158
    as shown by support for religion,
      131-32
    as shown by congressional
      support for prayer, 134
    as shown by selective use of
      history, 135-37
Sheppard, Nathaniel, Jr., 162
Sherman, Roger, 132
Shields, Carole, 55
Simon, Roger, 138
Skinner v. Railway Labor Executives' Assn., 92,
  93, 96
slavery, 64
Sontag, Susan, 66
Souter, David, 98, 129, 130
South Africa, 29, 31
South Carolina, 130, 131
Southern Baptist Convention, 121
Soviet Union, former, 31, 57
speech codes, 37, 41
  challenged by ACLU, 40
Spinello, Richard A., 79
Spinoza, Baruch (Benedict), 20

Stanford University, 28
Starr, Kenneth, 149
Stevens, John Paul, 98
St. Matthew Evangelical Lutheran
  Church and Schools (Milwaukee),
  151
Strossen, Nadine, 31, 65
Sunstein, Cass R., 81
Supreme Court, U.S., 44, 56, 60
  and ban on school prayer, 140, 143
  in Chaplinsky v. New Hampshire, 39
  and exceptions to protected speech,
    173
  on freedom of press, 82
  interpretation of First Amendment,
    66, 67
  on obscenity, 169, 178
    and Internet, 177
  in R.A.V. v. St. Paul, 40
  and Reno v. ACLU decision, 175, 177
  on separation of church and state,
    129-30
  on teenagers' access to information,
    181
  on wiretaps, 108
Swaggart, Jimmy, 139

Taxpayer Identification Number, 80
technology, 186, 190
Ten Commandments, 143
terrorism, 113, 116
Texas, 140, 148
Theme Is Freedom: Religion, Politics, and the
  American Tradition, The (Evans), 128
Thomas, Clarence, 89
Thompson, Tommy, 149
Time, 51
Tokyo, 74
Traynor, Charles, 61
Treasury Employees v. Von Raab, 96
Truett, George W., 121, 122
Turiano, Mark, 22

Unabomber, 112, 116
Under God (Wills), 123
United Kingdom, 40, 54, 123, 125,
  130
  child pornography in, 62
  laws to limit pornography, 60-63
    as appropriate sacrifice of freedom,
      64
  and separation of church and state, 124
United States, 31, 34, 43, 62, 193
  Congress, 76, 78, 131, 132, 133
    on flag burning, 139
  House Judiciary Committee, 108
    and regulation of medical data, 165
  Constitution, 19, 50, 130, 190

amendment provided for in, 51
Bill of Rights, should not be
  amended, 55-56
civil rights guaranteed by, 107
First Amendment of, 31, 37, 48, 49,
  53
  different versions of, 120
  and Founding Fathers, 17, 20, 126
  is for everyone, including bigots,
    38, 41
  and James Madison, 135
  as less valuable to minority than
    majority, 33
  as obstacle in civil rights era, 32
  as prohibition against federal
    government, 134
  and religion, 136, 137
  use of nonverbal symbols not
    protected by, 39-40
  and prayer, 132, 143
  and proposal to eliminate aid to
    Catholic schools, 155
  on right to privacy, 92-93, 102,
    106, 190, 194
  and compelling-interest
    exceptions, 96-97
  and law, 87
  and press, 83
  in schools, 94-95
  various ways of interpreting, 78
  as symbolic document, 47
  as symbolized by flag, 46
Justice Department, 110, 184
as land of free speech, 54
private schools in, 156
slavery in, 64
see also Court of Appeals, U.S.; Supreme
  Court, U.S.
United States v. Martinez Fuerte, 94, 100
United States v. Montoya de Hernandez, 100
University of California at Berkeley, 28,
  29
University of Chicago, 81
University of Connecticut, 40

University of Massachusetts, 28
University of Michigan, 40
University of Texas, 28-29
University of Wisconsin, 28, 40
USA Today, 154

vaccinations, 94, 103
Vernonia School District (Oregon). See
  under random drug tests
Virginia, 124, 125, 136, 169
  Constitutional Convention in, 126

Waco, Texas, incident, 109
Wall Street Journal, 155
Washington, 141, 150
Washington, George, 134, 135,
  190
Washington Post, 49, 140
Wayner, Peter, 189
Welch, Shyla, 169
welfare system, 74
Well of Loneliness (Hall), 60
White House, 175, 177
Whittle, Chris, 157, 158
Why Pornography Should Not Be Censored
  (Grey), 68
Williams, Annette "Polly," 151
Williams, Roger, 124-25, 126
Wills, Garry, 123
Wired magazine, 192
wiretaps, 113
  increasing use of, 109
  and new technology, 110
  privacy violated by, 107, 108, 111,
    113, 114
  as protection/crime-fighting devices,
    112, 115, 116
Wisconsin
  and Milwaukee school-voucher
    programs, 147-52
  Policy Research Institute of, 149
World Wide Web, 163

Yun, David, 27